NAVIGATING THE COYOTES IN OUR PRESENCE

Navigating The Coyotes In Our Presence

R.A. ZILIANT

LUMINARE PRESS
WWW.LUMINAREPRESS.COM

Navigating The Coyotes In Our Presence
Copyright © 2020 by R.A. Ziliant

All rights reserved. This book or any portion thereof may not be reproduced or used in any manner whatsoever without the express written permission of the publisher, except for the use of brief quotations in a book review.

Printed in the United States of America

Cover Artwork by Rose Twardowski
Book Layout by Nina Leis

Luminare Press
442 Charnelton St.
Eugene, OR 97401
www.luminarepress.com

LCCN: 2020913583
ISBN: 978-1-64388-423-3

To my Angels

Introduction

SURVIVORS ARE AS ADAPTABLE AS THEIR PREDATORS!

The inspiration for the title came about as a result of an encounter with a *Canis latrans* (coyote) while I was out for a morning jog. (Translated, *Canis latrans* means barking dog.) It was a typical summer morning; in order to beat the heat and humidity, I left home early. I had just turned the corner to head downhill when out of the field to my right a coyote ran right in front of me! I stopped dead in the middle of the road; the coyote stopped as well. We stood there—like a couple of gun-slingers waiting for the other to move. I could turn around and run back home or I could continue towards the coyote; either way it would catch me. I ran towards the coyote and it turned tail and ran back into the field. As I ran by, it sat in the field watching me. This was odd behavior coming from an animal that generally is extremely cautious. I picked up my pace because I didn't know why it was watching me! Once I was at a safe distance, I remembered a recent conversation I had about the mythological coyote. As a survivor of early childhood sexual abuse, I had been kicking around the idea of a book and thought what a great idea to use the coyote metaphorically. I began the process of researching coyotes and the result is this book, a profound twist on a devastating subject.

The coyotes represent the predators (child molesters, pedophiles, rapists and abusers) in our lives. I discovered that the coyote is an opportunistic predator—meaning it eats what is readily available and takes only what comes easily. It will take down a weak animal and tear it to shreds. If nursing, it will regurgitate food for its young. But, interestingly, coyotes typically go for smaller animals such as field mice (small and vulnerable). Sound familiar? How many of us are victims of this opportunism?

The coyote is revered by many Native American tribes as well as the Aztecs where it is believed that the mythology of the coyote began. "The Navajo refer to the coyote as God's Dog." (Ryden, xiii) The Crow's beliefs lend credence to the subject of this book; "they believed that the coyote was supreme and cast the coyote in the various roles of transformer, trickster and fool." (Ryden, xii) Most of us are keenly aware of how the transformer and trickster play a key role in our lives. For many survivors, unfortunately, these roles may be played by our family members.

Throughout this endeavor, I will elaborate on the transformer and trickster aspects of the coyote because they do play a key role. I would also like to note that coyotes have been referred to as "ghosts of the forest" (Grady, 14) and as survivors we know that these predators haunt us for the rest of our lives. The Apaches' belief further solidifies the metaphoric premise of this book because they believed "that in pre-human times Coyote created a path in which man is doomed to follow—a path of gluttony, lying, theft, adultery and other wrongdoings." (Dobie, 266) According to the Apache, "Coyote did first what man does now." (Dobie, 266)

As coyote mythology spread throughout the north, the Native Americans began to call him the Trickster. "The coyote is gullible, greedy and forgetful; a thief who loses or abuses what it steals." The coyote is known as a mischief-maker and can transform itself into any shape it wants." (Grady, 74, 75) "Coyote, the animal, is as complex and opportunistic as Coyote the Trickster was in the legends. The coyote's trickster ability to change into whatever form suited the occasion, is mirrored in the coyote's adaptability to any environment it finds itself in." (Grady, 76)

Interesting - if we consider how predators operate; they are greedy, and abuse us while stealing our innocence. Additionally, I cannot stress enough how opportunistic predators are. They rely on the gullibility of their victims. The lack of a predator's empathy lends to the belief that their actions have little or no impact on their victims. It is this characteristic that allows them to deny accountability. The combination of the predator's characteristics and that of their victim are equally culpable and cannot be stressed enough.

Despite the fact that coyotes are often and easily killed by hunters, trappers and farmers, they continue to come back in greater numbers and are able to prosper in close proximity to us. The coyote's adaptability is especially relevant because it mirrors the infiltration of predators today despite new regulations and public awareness. Additionally, human predators are aided by the internet and social media outlets, which makes navigating coyotes that much more difficult.

Spotting a coyote is a rare occurrence despite their population. If you are fortunate or unfortunate (depending on your perspective) to happen upon one, the Native Americans see it as a sign of a new beginning or end, hence a new beginning. My run in with the coyote paralleled my life at the time. As I try to begin a new life, thereby ending my old or vice versa the question becomes, do I have the same survival instincts as those who pursue me? Can I successfully navigate the coyotes in my presence?

Writing about abuse is probably the hardest thing for a survivor to do. It can take an average of 20 years for a survivor to actually divulge what happened! Even today as I write this, it is difficult to put down in words what happened to me. It is painful, shameful, nauseating, and extremely uncomfortable, and there is a lot of anger to resolve. I find myself keeping a distance between my past and present. You may notice throughout this memoir that I seem somewhat detached emotionally from events or interactions and that is because I am unable to articulate my feelings even today… there are 'things' I will never talk about.

Writing about what happened is supposed to put distance between us and the past. I understand the concept. If I can write about it then it isn't really hurting me—right? The typical phrase is that the predator can't hurt you now. I agree up to a point. What they are really referring to is the physical pain. But there is pain - - it does hurt me now. Every decision I was either forced to make or made, was based on lies or half-truths. The effects of that continue to influence me today. All my built-in defenses are a double-edged sword. What helped me get through the abuse has inhibited my growth as an adult—I'm stuck until my thought processes change.

The most prevalent thought and/or feeling I had then and still do to some degree even today is that—everyone knows! I remember specifically thinking that there was something wrong with me and others could see it or knew it somehow; like there was a sign on my head that says I'm damaged goods. Obviously this makes me extremely self-conscious. To others, I'm a bitch, anti-social or snobby but in reality, I am scared to death that people can see the real me; the abused me and the truth about my sick family. I carry around shame; it is my cross to bear. In reality it is nothing more than a disability that won't allow me to love myself or see who I am. This book, I hope, is an exercise or more accurately an exorcism of the pain, guilt, shame and anger.

Chapter 1

"Dens are typically dug by the female and are well hidden. The female is the only one to enter a den and that is to give birth. They vacate the den once the pups are ready to disperse. It is a misconception that coyotes live in dens. They sleep on the open ground or day beds—made by turning around a few dozen times to press down the grass or snow, behavior observed in domestic dogs." (Grady, 33) I use the term den in this chapter as it relates to my birth and the period in which the alpha pair (parents) are nurturing and raising their pups (children) to be young responsible pack members.

My den consisted of my parents (Joe and Colleen), two younger siblings (Jeff and Bill) and myself. We lived in a typical middle-class neighborhood in Albany. I used to walk to Catholic school. When I was 7, we moved to a small town in the countryside. My parents bought an old farm house built in the mid-1800s on 50 acres.

Joe was one of five boys, of French-Canadian and German background. He was a handsome man who kept to himself most of the time. Joe wasn't much of a communicator unless he was yelling. As I grew older, I discovered that he had quite an adventurous side as well. But as a young child, in my eyes, he was mean. Memories of my father are mostly negative. I remember a lot of yelling, hitting, and beatings. I cannot recall any good memories from that period in my life—not one. If I were to take an educated guess, my father was the typical coyote.

Once we moved, he pretty much stayed to himself—meaning he would come home from work and sit in his recliner, watch the idiot box as he called it, and smoke his cigarettes. He didn't participate in activities with his children on any level. It was very rare for him to take an interest in me or my brothers unless he needed our help with renovations in the house. When I say our, I really mean my help. My father never had much use for the boys. My grandmother had five boys and in my opinion, made them feel inferior because she wanted a girl so badly. No one seems to know if the grandparents beat them.

Basically, we kids were on our own with zero support. That was the father I knew most of the time. He had another side, which was only on display when he was with friends or drinking. With them he was friendly. He laughed and bragged about his shenanigans in the Navy. He talked about his trip to Alaska with the one-eyed pilot and how they ran out of gas over the Yukon and had to make an emergency landing, but did so without clearing it with the Canadian authorities. They were promptly arrested when they landed! He would also talk about his trip to the Indy 500.

When Joe was in high school his car was hit head on by a dump truck. As the story goes, he was resuscitated at the scene. My grandparents sued and won a huge settlement. My father thought that it should have gone to him, but my grandmother took the money for herself. Then Joe promptly signed up for a tour in the Navy. For as long as I can remember, my father barely spoke to my grandparents; it didn't matter if we were at a family function. In fact, I can count on one hand how many times he called them mom and dad. When my grandparents visited for the holidays, my father would sit in his recliner and not say one word to his parents. Looking back on it now, knowing my father, he was sitting there all consumed with hate.

Colleen, my mother, is Irish and Native Canadian Indian. I would say she was pretty like Cher in the day but not as thin. My mother is a piece of work. What can I say. In order to escape my abusive father, she had multiple affairs which Jeff and I were witness to. She is self-absorbed, gullible (in the coyote sense) and a pathological liar, in my opinion. She is the ultimate narcissist. The emotional abuse we suffered at the hands of my mother surpasses all the physical abuse my father could dish out. Having said that, she was, however, more involved in our lives but her interest was fleeting. She had children, but didn't want the responsibility. She was like that with her animals too. She would bring all sorts of stray cats, dogs and birds home, but then she would lose interest and not take care of them. My brothers, the house, and the animals inevitably became my responsibility.

Colleen lost her mother at the age of twelve to cancer. She actually held her dying mother in her arms while they were waiting for an ambulance that arrived too late. My grandmother had a heart attack brought on by the cancer as she was getting into the car for church. My mother was one of six siblings (one sister and four brothers), four of whom were much older than she was. So she and her younger brother were left with a very old-fashioned and stubborn Irish father. They were separated for a while and sent to live with their older brothers.

My grandfather quickly remarried a woman my grandmother had absolutely hated. The woman was mean and she would put the moves on my grandfather at their restaurant. My grandparents owned a bakery/restaurant that was passed down through the generations but was ultimately sold when my grandmother became too ill. After my grandfather remarried, my mother and uncle were brought back to live with them. In the meantime, my grandfather had thrown out everything that reminded him of my grandmother. This was his way of dealing with the pain of losing her. My mother was never allowed to talk about her either. Anyway, the stepmom was of storybook nature—as in Cinderella. She hated my mother and uncle. My aunt and uncles would have nothing to do with her.

Joe, recently back from his tour in the Navy was working as a soda jerk (reserving all comments here) for his parents at their dairy bar in Albany. The bar happened to be a few blocks from where my uncle's (Colleen's brother's) pharmacy was. My mother had been working for him since she was twelve delivering medicine and working in the store. So Joe and Colleen met at the dairy bar where my father was serving up ice cream and soda floats. He was five years her senior—she was eighteen. They married when she turned nineteen. I was a honeymoon baby, born exactly nine months to the day. My grandfather was keeping an eye on the calendar. Had I been born sooner, he would have killed my father!

The following year Jeff was born. His arrival was a little more dramatic. My father came home drunk one night and an argument ensued. He pushed my mother down a flight of stairs forcing her into labor. Jeff was born three months premature. Back then, preemies didn't have much of a chance, but he survived and I think on some level my father hated him for that. You would think that surviving would garner some respect, but not from Joe. Jeff suffered constant bronchitis for the first five or six years of his life as his lungs were underdeveloped.

Joe and Colleen were a match made in heaven! But seriously, they both wreaked havoc upon us with zero concern for any effects. Isn't that what the coyote is all about? To be fair, coyotes are good parents. Coyotes do an excellent job of rearing their young - preparing them for life in the cruel world that awaits them. What were my parents preparing us for? To be fair, my father did have his moments when his instinct to protect us kicked in. Unfortunately, his temper would get the better of him and it wasn't always a pretty scene.

For years I was convinced that the person who sexually abused me was the man that watched us when my mother was working. You see, I always remembered the incidents of abuse but I have blocked out the face, even to this day. I was in my forties when I found out that this man was a friend of my father's who stayed with us for about a year. It could have been either one of them. Not only that, but it may have been the both of them, my father and his friend. I thought I was going to die right on the spot when my therapist said that out loud. The abuser could also have been one of my mother's many lovers—no way of knowing. The fact that I can't see the face plays into my worst fears. Not to mention the fact that I still can't stand the smell of scotch, as it was on the breath of my abuser, and is therefore unforgettable. It's been said that the brain will not allow us to see what we can't handle. I have a hard time recognizing my father as the one who abused me. A part of me still wants it to be the "other" guy!

One day, like any other day in my early childhood, my mother took us to the grocery store were we would meet her lover and park in one of the shopping center's lots. Jeff and I had grown accustomed to sitting in our car while the two of them had sex in her lover's car, which was parked right next to us. I'm sure we couldn't have been there for more than a typical lunch hour but to us it seemed like an eternity.

One day the boyfriend took us to lunch at McDonald's. It was the first time we had ever been there. The excitement of such an adventure was overwhelming especially to me. Our parents never took us anywhere. To go to a place with big golden arches and a clown was beyond my wildest imagination. So the excitement of the day overflowed into the evening hours when my father arrived home. As I rattled off to him about going there, my excitement got the better of me and I slipped and mentioned we were there with the man. He asked what man and I said, you know the man. He looked at my mother and she started to cry. My father had an explosive personality; you never knew what would set him off and it didn't take much. If he were drinking, there would be hell to pay. He grabbed Jeff and beat him and I mean beat him. He was yelling at my mother to tell him who she was with and all she could do was cry. She wouldn't do anything to help Jeff who at that point was screaming and crying so loudly I thought my ears would pop.

As I covered my ears and looked frantically at her and then back at my father who was still beating the hell out of Jeff, I knew I had to take control or Jeff was going to be a bloody mess. I shouted out, you know the man in the suit! Ronald McDonald! Despite my vulnerability, it was at that moment I knew I had taken control and become the parent. The funny thing is I never really took advantage because my father was so explosive, I didn't dare. Jeff and I walked on eggshells always. Both of us were terrified of my father's beatings.

On another occasion while sitting in the car, I saw a truck that looked like my father's drive by. When my mother got back in the car, I told her that I had seen dad's truck. After that, the couple switched the location where we would park, alternating parking lots so as not to be found out. One time we went to her lover's house. They sat us on the floor in the living room to watch TV while they went upstairs to have sex.

Jeff and I would always watch them when we were in the car. They thought we couldn't see what was going on but when you are four, five, six, going on seven years old, what else is there to do but watch? Every time I think about it I wonder, what the hell was going through her mind. If someone did that today, they would be arrested for leaving their kids in the car or worse. Not to mention watching the porn show on the side. What an education we received. Think about it. She was giving us a show almost on a daily basis, while I was simultaneously being sexually abused. What was the lesson for me? On occasion guys would come to the house, but oddly enough they weren't the same guy she saw on a daily basis. Not sure who they were; it's probably best that I didn't know.

One evening when my mother was working, my abuser looked at me and said "your mother is at work - that means we can play!" I knew what that meant and as I started to run for cover in my bedroom, he grabbed me from behind and dragged me back. To this day, I swear it is why I don't like people coming up behind me. I remember very specific details, but the face has always eluded me. The man watched us during the day too. He would tell my brother to go outside and play, then take me into the bedroom. On several occasions he would lay me down so that I was partially under the bed. If it was my brother's room, he would place me partially under the cot, which had a steel bar that ran across the floor. Even now whenever I am under severe stress my back aches in that spot. He would do things to me and then ask me do things to him. He would say "It's a game. Think of it as a lollipop!" For the longest time I refused to eat a Dum Dum, and when the Tootsie Pop commercial came out, I was like, forget about it! I know what is in the center.

One night when Joe came home drunk, he and my mother argued. He beat her, ripped her nightgown off, ripped the phone off the wall, and put a hole through the door. I woke to hear her screaming. I went and grabbed Jeff from his room and ran to the kitchen only to see my mother standing there naked with a butcher knife in one hand and a wicker laundry basket in the other. Using the basket as a shield, she was fending off my father as he lunged towards her. She yelled at us to get behind her. My father had his bow and arrow pointed directly at my mother. Before my father ripped the phone of the wall my mother had called her sister. My uncle drove over with my cousin and she walked in on them. She screamed at my father to drop the bow.

During another argument, my mother managed to get us out of the house and into the car. She drove to my aunt's house, which was a good half-hour away. She ran to the front door and knocked until my uncle answered. When he answered, my mother was standing there buck naked! Sadly, that wasn't the first time we arrived at my aunt's in that fashion.

Jeff and I spent a lot of time at my Aunt Ann and Uncle's John's. In fact, it was our second home and the only source of "normalcy" we knew. After I was born, my parents lived with them for almost a year. It was never clear why. My aunt was pregnant with my cousin when I was born. She delivered four months later, but my cousin died three days after. My aunt spoiled me as a result. She had two older daughters, so they always babysat for my mother and took me everywhere they went.

My parents eventually rented an old farmhouse not far from them. Shortly after, Joe and Colleen had a clambake during which a tornado hit. Everything in the area was down including power lines and trees. My aunt and uncle loved to tell this story because my father and his friends were so loaded that they were swinging from the downed power lines like monkeys. Everyone was standing in the front window watching them and my mother was hoping the power would go on.

In addition to drinking, smashing things, beating us and well, acting like a monkey, my father would get out his bow and arrow and shoot the neighbor's cats. He didn't like cats and they had a lot of them so he figured it was okay to knock a few of them off. In spite of the fact that he didn't like animals, we always had a dog unless he killed it, which he often did.

And if there weren't enough problems already, my mother got pregnant. I don't remember much of the pregnancy. No one believes Joe is actually the father. Bill doesn't look anything like us. He does look like my mother's boyfriend at the time. Years later when my parents divorced, my father asked for a paternity test, my mother refused.

On one occasion the family took a trip to the mountains to visit my father's Navy buddy. This trip stands out because it is one of only a few my parents ever took. We used my aunt and uncle's convertible to go. My father who was in the Navy couldn't swim and neither could my mother. I was out on a log with his friend's kids, they rolled the log and I went under. I didn't know how to swim, so I held on until I couldn't. I nearly drowned in the lake! Joe's friend ended up going in after me. I remember lying on the beach with them standing over me. They covered me in blankets and that's all I remember.

Back home one evening we were sitting at the kitchen table. My mother was serving spaghetti. She was placing our servings on our plates and talking at the same time. As she handed me my plate, it tilted. The hot spaghetti sauce ran down me and my clothes! My father jumped up from his end of the table and ran over to me and ripped my robe and nightgown off. I had first degree burns on my hand. My hand was one big giant blister. I couldn't even see my hand, just my fingers jutting out of this blister. The next morning I had school. Everyone stared at me.

Around this time I started running away. Joe and Colleen had been fighting (I can't remember about what) and I packed my suitcase and left the house. Naturally I didn't get far, how far is a six year old going? But, it was the beginning of a long trend. Whenever the situation became violent or I felt cornered, I would run.

Before moving to the country, something happened. I have horrible dreams of not being able to breathe. I apparently fell down a flight of stairs. I lost my front teeth and I went a long time without them. I think it has something to do with my abuser and the lollipop because I remember refusing.

Chapter 2

The Pack: Typically consists of three to eight coyotes with an average pack size of 6. The pack consists of the alpha pair (mating pair) and two or more beta coyotes. The beta coyotes protect the pack and pups - they are permanent members (pups who have not dispersed by November after birth). The coyote social structure is very important as they rely on strong family bonds and shared territories for survival. (Grady, 31, 32)

When I was seven, my father moved us from the city to the country; from a new house that my parents built to an old farmhouse built in the mid-1800s. It was run-down but had a lot of property, so much in fact, that our property, fifty acres, encompassed both sides of the road and down the hill to the next intersection, which was a dirt crossroad. We lived on the only paved section. The house had a big hole in the roof. Although it was never mentioned why we moved there, my father hinted over the years that it had everything to do with my mother. On the few occasions when I tried to get answers about my past from him he would say, ask your mother. Asking her and expecting the truth was an exercise in futility. When I did ask, she said ask your father so I never found out the truth about the move. To this day, I am convinced it was his way of punishing my mother.

The sexual abuse stopped, but the drinking and physical abuse continued. Our first winter there was torture. The well constantly ran dry and the power went out on a regular basis. We were running to the neighbor's for jugs of water. We didn't have walls in some rooms and Jeff was constantly sick with bronchitis. In fact, during the winter, a severe snowstorm hit dumping so much snow that my father couldn't get home from the city. Jeff was so sick that my mother had to call the doctor in the middle of the night. He told her to build an oxygen tent over Jeff and the fire department had someone on a snowmobile drive out to our house to deliver medicine. That spring a new roof was put on and my father started to gut and remodel the house.

On Christmas Eve following our move, I woke to screaming and yelling. I got up and went to the top of the stairs; I heard my uncle and cousin below. As I walked downstairs I could hear them sweeping and cleaning up glass. The kitchen table was broken in two and broken glass from the dishes Joe had smashed were everywhere. Joe had come home drunk from his company Christmas party and Colleen never knew when to shut her mouth. You can't argue with a drunk, but she did and he beat her and smashed everything in sight.

Christmas morning I sat in the living room in front of the tree wondering what was going to go down. My mother refused to open any gifts and my father lay there half comatose from a hangover insisting that we open our gifts. My grandparents, Joe's parents, were supposed to come for dinner, but obviously my mother didn't want them there. She called and told them a story. They showed up a few hours later to see what was going on. My mother answered the door sporting a swollen face and black eye.

After moving to the "farm" as my father commonly referred to it (even though it wasn't a working one), Colleen started to take in stray cats despite the fact that Joe hated them. Everyone knew when he got mad, something or someone would get beaten or even worse. He would beat us, but when he was really pissed off, he would shoot one of the animals just to watch my mother cry. I never understood her. Why would you bring an animal home, knowing full well the probability of the end result?

Additionally, she started to hoard clothes. We always received hand-me-downs from the family. We have a huge extended Irish family and since my mother's siblings were so much older than her, they would give her clothes, toys, and all kinds of things. When my parents were first married, my father was going to school part time and worked as a pipe fitter apprentice so money was tight. But when he started to make good money, she continued the poverty act. She did it to play the victim and to attract men. She had lots of nice clothes, but instead would put them in big green garbage bags and store them in her closet and wear rags around.

God forbid if we needed clothes; we were allowed to shop twice a year, once for the beginning of the school year and a few things for summer. She would buy us the minimum. I was constantly washing my clothes because she would only buy 5 pairs of underwear and socks and that had to last the whole year. She never asked if we needed anything. The only time she would spend real money on clothes was for Easter. Every year, we had to have new Easter outfits. Again, I could never understand her logic.

My mother was the same way when I started my period. She would never ask if I needed anything—she didn't want to know, so I would have to scrounge around for whatever she had in the house. It was never discussed between us. It was as if my needs had no importance. The topic of sex was never discussed and it was just as well. It was uncomfortable considering I used to watch her and her men together. I was grossed out.

For the first couple of years in the new old house, my mother tried to be active in our lives. She was working on the marriage though she continued to see her lover. Not sure how you work on a marriage while still having an affair, but she tried.

Colleen became a Brownie leader and den mother, but the most hypocritical thing she did was to become our religious education instructor. Yes, she was my Sunday school teacher; we were raised Catholic. Every Sunday she would pretend to be a saint. Talk about trickster. And, adding insult to injury she actually took it seriously too. I would watch her prepare for her lessons. She had her bible and reference books, and would carry this big cross with her. She loved the holier than thou bit. She should have been a teacher because she loved preaching. Before meeting Joe, she went to a convent to become a NUN! Apparently she didn't like it. My classmates loved her. They thought she was cool.

The curious thing is that I loved going to church! I loved everything about it, the smell, the formality and structure of it all. When you don't have a sense of belonging church becomes a refuge. And, for me, I had no sense of belonging. The only place I felt safe, other than church, was at my aunt and uncle's. I knew I was different (damaged); I didn't fit in at school. I pretty much went my own way most of the time. I would lie awake at night praying to whomever or whatever was out there for help. There was something spooky in the old house. I think it was a good spirit, but there was definitely something.

Joe was totally missing in action when it came to church or anything remotely related to faith but that changed later in his life. One of the few times I do remember Joe attending any mass was for my first communion. I knew it was a big deal for Joe to dress in a suit and the family came to the house afterward for a party. I always felt awkward at family events back then; I felt mostly embarrassed or out of place. Anyway, the day turned out to be a fiasco. The actual ceremony went well. It was what happened afterward that resonates in my mind. The party was at the house, which was probably the first time many of the relatives had been to the "farmhouse." Even my grandfather (Colleen's father) was there. He didn't attend many family functions because no one liked my step-grandmother.

My father was out in the yard giving the guys a tour (he was drinking quite heavily) and everything seemed to be going well. My cousins and I decided to take a walk and took the youngest cousin with us. She was six months old. My brother Jeff was at the top of the hill as we walked passed him; he was tossing stones out into the field. One of the stones hit the six-month old in the head and she cried. Blood was running down her head. We ran back to the house and into the kitchen to grab a towel to clean her off. It wasn't a big gash, but enough to scare her. My father heard all the commotion and came running into the house to find out what happened. By this time dusk was settling in.

When my father found out Jeff was throwing stones and one hit the baby, he went crazy! My father grabbed him and started to beat him with a large stick he had cut from a tree earlier in the day. He wailed on him and to this day I remember everyone and I mean EVERYONE there yelling for him to stop. My grandfather (the stubborn-old Irishman) was standing there, my mother's brothers (lawyers, judges and doctors), my father's parents, they all stood there. They were afraid of my father. I watched as he beat my brother in front of the whole family. Eventually he let up and told Jeff to go to his room. The poor kid could barely stand up. It occurred to me, if these guys couldn't stop Joe, who could? Poor Jeff, such was his life at the hands of Joe and Colleen.

My mother had always worked part time but eventually took a full time job. By the age of nine it was my responsibility to take care of the house and have dinner on the table by the time Joe arrived home from work. I had to vacuum, dust, mop, clean the bathrooms, fix dinner, wash the dishes, do the laundry and somehow get my homework done. A year later, Colleen stopped waking us up for school and it was my responsibility to get us up and ready, including making lunches for my brothers and me.

By the time I was ten, I was drinking. No surprise there. I think the majority of abuse survivors do whatever they can to stay numb. I didn't drink every day, just when I needed to escape. My preference was whiskey. Still love it to this day and consume it for pleasure, albeit not as much. We all know what self-medication is. It is one of our many survival techniques.

When I wasn't drinking, compartmentalization also worked well. That was the first thing I learned to do because while you are being sexually abused, you pretend it isn't happening. The abuser ignores you until you are alone again, a vicious cycle, indeed. I refer to it as the invisible effect. In our house you might as well have been invisible. Harry Potter's invisible cape would have come in handy. At least I could have escaped.

Something else had started to happen in the farmhouse. I alluded to it earlier; I felt a presence and I would have dreams, very descriptive dreams about people or incidents that were premonitions.

During the summer months when being home was worse than hell, I spent hours in the woods designing and building forts. Not anything elaborate, just simple ones made out of fallen trees that my brothers and I would stack like Lincoln Logs. One of the cool things about the property was that it had several natural springs on it. We would build near a spring. We made some really good forts, one of which we used all the way through high school for various parties. I acquired my building skills from my father, who on the weekends would kick my butt out of bed at 5am to help remodel the house. He would hand me a wrecking bar and tell me to tear down a wall or we would build a new partition or install plumbing. I hated it because I would work all day and neither of my brothers was allowed to help. Bill was too young and well, Dad didn't like Jeff.

I remember an incident just before starting work on the old bathroom. I was standing in the dining room arguing with Joe, and my mother was there. Joe grabbed a broom and started beating me with the handle. I ran into the bathroom and locked the door, which was a mistake because you never locked my father out. He broke down the door and beat me all that much harder. My mother just stood there crying (her usual). He hit me so hard he broke the handle over my back! I hurt for days afterward and had bruises all over my back. Another time, he beat Jeff and me with his hunting belt using the big brass buckle, which left bloody welts.

One of my survival skills was to entrench myself in school. By the time I hit the eighth grade I was a straight A student and made the honor society. My mother had given up her boyfriend in the city, although they stayed in touch because of my brother Bill. She would take Bill into the city to visit with him periodically. She was gullible enough to think that slipped by me. In reality, she had already moved on and had a new lover. This one was her boss. It was a real predicament that didn't end well.

My father would come home from work, plop down in his chair, and watch TV. Never once did he ask how our day was, what we did in school or about extra-curricular activities or even support us in them. If we wanted to join a sports team or a club, not that we were encouraged to do so, we were on our own. We had to find our own way there and back. My mother was so self-absorbed that from the moment she arrived home, it was all about her. My father would just sit there, eat, nod his head, and mostly ignore her. We were never asked about our day or what we did unless we were in trouble for something. We ate as quickly as possible just to get away from the table. My brothers and I were invisible.

Shortly after finishing the remodeling of the first floor of the house (I was in the 6th grade), my brothers and I were out sledding for an afternoon. We lived on a hill and could start at the top and go for almost a quarter of mile on a good day. When that happened, it was a long walk back up the road. There was no way to walk back through all the snow. It was exhausting, so the road was the best option. After a few trips down the hill and back we headed home. We walked in through the front porch, where we left the sleds. We walked into the entry and started to take off our snow gear. Well, needless to say, we were covered in snow and it got all over the new carpet. Joe saw the snow and yelled at us. But he didn't let it go, he went into one of his rages and he grabbed me by my ankles as I sat on the floor taking off my boots. He held me upside down and rammed my head into the floor repeatedly while yelling about the snow. I saw stars. I went to my room afterwards and stayed there the rest of the night. I refused to eat dinner with my parents, which I did often to avoid them.

Already at a young age, boys were chasing me. In the fifth grade, one boy, William wanted to marry me. He was a cute blonde who sent me love letters and bottles of perfume in the mail. We had the same mailman, so William would give our mailman the gifts and asked him to leave them in my mailbox. The mailman thought it was sweet. I found it a little scary so I did my best to discourage him.

I was one of those girls who developed early; the other girls hated it and were cruel - a beat me up kind of cruel. I got into fights at school all the time. If I talked to a boy and a girl didn't like it, the girls would gang up on me outside. I was tough though, another survival skill I developed. To survive living with my father I had to be strong. Even though I was petite, I was able to hold my own, and I never backed down.

By the time I entered the eighth grade, I had "sex" (if that's what you would call it) with the neighbor boy, Sean, in the hayfield while playing hide-and-seek. Victims of early childhood sexual abuse often have sexual relations at a young age. Sean was a year older and all the girls were "in love" with him. He was an all-round jock, and played almost every sport the school offered. He had dark hair and the most beautiful dark long eyelashes and a pouty look when he wanted something. Sex was our little secret though. I was good at keeping secrets about sex. In public he ignored me and I was victimized again. The coyote had changed or shifted; being the trickster that he is. Instead of men abusing me, I had moved on to immature boys. So I played the game. We would have sex, Sean would ignore me, and I would ignore him. This is the adaptability part of the victim. Because I was so accustomed to compartmentalizing, I was able to block out his ignoring me and behave just like my abuser. Sean, on the other hand, being a teenage boy eventually bragged to all the guys. Word quickly spread and so I continued to get beaten upon by girls who felt intimidated. The funny thing is I still get along with men better than women. Women are too complicated. Do I include myself in that analysis? Absolutely.

With guys on the other hand, I always knew where I stood. I wasn't clingy or demanding. I would walk by the boys in the school hallways as if nothing ever happened (I was invisible) and they liked that. Remember, I was programmed to think sex was what you did with boys, period. They would also confide in me about their girlfriends, which landed me in all sorts of hot water because inevitably, one of the girls would get pissed and come looking to beat me up.

The summer before my eighth grade year was long and hot. I had become friends with the neighbor down the road, Stacey. She had horses and we would ride them through the fields and occasionally race. One particular summer day,

Stacey's brother had the idea to film a western movie. We would ride out into the fields and her brother, John, would film us. One day, we were out with the horses and decided to race through the fields. I had a different horse than I was used to riding. This horse was being stubborn and wouldn't let me tighten the saddle. As we raced, the saddle would loosen and slide sideways causing me to stop several times to tighten it.

As we rode across the field, Jeff was standing at the top of the hill throwing stones again. He spooked my horse and it took off like a bat out of hell. I tried to pull back on the reins but it wasn't working. The saddle slid all the way sideways and I went with it but my foot was caught in the stirrup. The horse dragged me across the field! He finally slowed as Stacey rode alongside me. Next thing I knew, Stacey's father was picking me up and carrying me out of the field. The horse had run home and her father spotted it wandering around. He jumped in his truck and came looking for us. I suffered a concussion. When my mother got home from work, she didn't even take me to the hospital.

Eighth grade was a very busy year for me. The coyotes were everywhere and it wasn't just the guys. Sean had become a huge liability. He lied about me and was jealous if someone else paid attention to me even as he ignored me in front of his friends.

Two major events happened that year. At the beginning of the school year, I had secured a position with the boys' basketball coach as an office helper. A few weeks later, I brought a friend, Shelly, into the office and she too was asked to help out. Now Shelly was well-endowed, and she was also one of the toughest people I knew. Although we never discussed it, she had it worse than me. Her father beat the crap out of her, her sisters and their mother. He was one S.O.B. The girls were cowgirls on the rodeo circuits. He worked them hard. They did whatever he said or else.

Shelly and I worked in the office during our lunch time or would stay after school to do clerical work like mailing flyers. We would get silly from time to time and joke around with the coach. We also took turns babysitting for his family. It was a small town and everyone knew everyone. So we knew the teachers outside of school.

Well, Sean decided to tell his father that we were having sex with the coach, and all hell broke loose. We were brought to the school superintendent for questioning. My parents had to attend a board meeting and the coach was brought up on false charges. I was adamant that he never touched me and he didn't! We were told we could no longer work for the coach and he was forbidden to have girls help out in the office. This had been a tradition with him; every year he had an eighth grader help out. Sean ruined the coach's life! The coach had to eventually move out of town. Given this unfortunate experience, I'm very cautious about jumping to conclusions when sexual abuse accusations are thrown around until all evidence is presented. I've been on both sides.

A firestorm started because after that, no one believed us, and the guys in school were looking to get laid. If I even looked at a guy, I would get punched by an angry girlfriend. It created a very unstable environment in school for Shelly and me, which ultimately led to the next event when I was accused of chasing another girl's boyfriend. I had a conversation with him, about her actually. The girlfriend, Pam, confronted me and told me to stop talking to him. I said that that was ridiculous, I can talk to anyone I want. She asked me to meet her outside after school so

I prepared myself for yet another fight. I was cornered by Pam who had a knife in her hand. She threatened to stab me if I didn't stay away from her boyfriend. I told my father what happened and he exploded. For once he acted like a father. He went to the school the next day and argued with the principal. Joe scared the hell out of him because Pam was suspended from school. It was one hell of a way to end my eighth grade school year.

In school the only escape I had was the ski club. It took a lot of begging to get my parents to agree. I used the "I do all the chores and don't get paid approach." What a lifesaver the club was. I looked forward to Saturdays during ski season. It meant one entire day away from home, doing what I enjoyed. No work, refereeing, unpredictable outbursts, or dealing with my mother and her illicit affairs. Saturdays gave me the opportunity to pretend for eight hours that I was a normal person.

The summer before my freshman year, I babysat for my cousin on and off. I was the only one she trusted with her four kids; the youngest was six-months old. Everyone commented on how mature I was because they all knew what my responsibilities were at home. My cousin who is much older than me (on my mother's side) had asked me to babysit for her so she could attend a wedding. She and her husband had planned on a three-day weekend.

My cousin's husband picked me up and as we drove to their house, he turned down a side road, pulled the car over and started telling me how my cousin wouldn't have anything to do with him anymore. Then he grabbed me, started kissing me, tried putting his hand down my pants, and tried to remove my bra. As I fought him, he kept repeating that my cousin wouldn't have anything to do with him. Then he started to cry, and I ended up consoling him. I was at an age when older men started to have an interest in me. My cousin's husband wasn't the last. I also had a local sheriff, of all people, chasing me as well. He spotted me hanging laundry one day and stopped by to ask if I needed any assistance. He drove by the house often after that. At what point do you say to yourself, there a sign above my head that says come on in? The transformer coyotes were everywhere.

Around this time, I had my first experience with an older man. Talk about ruining the image of being the "responsible one." One of my best friends, Diane, had an older brother ten years my senior. We met one night while I was visiting her. He was in their barn shooting pool with a friend. We went out to shoot some pool; Diane had a crush on his friend. So we shot some pool, smoked cigarettes and a couple of joints. Diane went off to be alone with the other guy; mind you, he was ten years her senior as well and married. I was left alone with Rob. I remember that night like it was yesterday. He looked like Jesus with his long dark curly hair and he had a wicked laugh. He had an old department store utility van, all beat to shit, but it was his make-out van. He took me to the van where we made out. Thankfully he drew the line at sex.

What a crazy summer! I would sneak out at night and go out with Rob and his buddies. Diane would meet up with her new man. One night, we went to a party. There was a huge bonfire and placed strategically in the fire were bottles of gasoline. To say Rob was a daredevil would be an understatement. There wasn't anything he wouldn't try. Rob decided it would be a good idea to jump over the fire. As we watched him leap back and forth, the last time he jumped, he just cleared the fire when one of the bottles exploded.

The bonfire flared sky high. Then another bottle went off. He came so close to having his balls blown off, but he stood there laughing that wicked laugh.

We were out partying one night and the crazy bastard took us to a road with a bridge that was under construction. The whole middle section was gone; Rob turned the van around, drove back to the intersection, turned around again and floored the gas. We hit the dirt pile just ahead of the road block and were airborne, just clearing the section that was out. Honestly, he loved to scare the shit out of people (mostly girls) because he would get off on hearing us scream. The louder you screamed, the more he would laugh that wicked laugh.

One beautiful summer day he stopped by and asked if I wanted to ride with him to the city to get some car parts. Of course, I said yes because he had me hook, line, and sinker. Anytime I went with him, I knew it was going to be an adventure. That day I ended up with a very bad sunburn as I hadn't considered what would happen on a motorcycle wearing a tube top and shorts. Ouch. That summer opened me up to a world that teetered precariously between life and death and I didn't care. I just wanted out and it didn't matter how.

The beginning of my freshman year was anything but typical. My drinking or self-medication had increased. I was smoking, which also included the occasional joint. I missed the first couple of weeks of school because I was in the hospital with my back which had been giving me problems. My parents had called a specialist. After several tests and days in the hospital, the specialist told them it was all in my head. Looking back on it now, it was probably an accurate assessment. During the sexual abuse, my back was pushed onto a steel bar so whenever I'm under stress my back bothers me.

    Like any typical freshman I was stressed about entering the ninth grade. However, my stress was exponentially greater than the typical freshman. My reputation was abysmal, and I had no support at home and no idea what to expect. In addition, my strange dreams were increasing as well as the inexplicable incidents in the old farmhouse. Like hearing someone walk down the hallway and stop at the door. I would open the door and no one would be there. This happened to my brothers as well. The three of us would be in our bedrooms and our parents downstairs when a door would slam loudly. In our house everyone would run to see what happened because with my father you never knew. We would insist that the noise came from the downstairs and our parents would say it came from the upstairs. I would walk into the living room where no one was sitting and the rocking chair would be rocking. One time when I was home alone, I was taking a shower and heard a door open and shut. I thought one of the boys had come home. When I got out and went to the living room, the rocker was rocking and a cigarette was burning in the ashtray, but no one was in the house. I ran back into the bathroom and locked the door and waited for someone to come home.

    One particularly weird experience happened after visiting a so called haunted house down the road. It was off on a dirt path, hidden by dozens of trees. Legend has it a boy was playing in the barn and accidently hung himself while swinging on a rope from the rafters. The farmhouse had been abandoned and all but two barns remained standing. The rest of the structures had collapsed onto their foundations. Walking around the grounds gave me goose bumps.

I walked past what looked to be old stone graves but they were probably portions of an old stone wall. When you are kids, you make up imaginary things in your head. Jeff, who was with me, and I picked up an old bottle and used it as a talisman. We said that if it broke, we would be haunted for the rest of our lives. The bottle broke on the walk back. When I woke the next morning, there were crosses drawn all over the curtains in my room. They weren't random either; some were in groups that formed shapes. I ran out of my room yelling for my mother to come and look at the curtains. I blamed my brothers for the crosses, but there was no way they could have done what was there. We never figured out how the crosses got there and I couldn't wash them out because they were done in ink.

I survived my freshman year mostly intact. A few minor skirmishes, but all in all, most everyone was on their best behavior. I was in homework overload taking all upper-level classes and three majors. Between trying to maintain my "A" status and the work at home, I didn't have much time to get into trouble. Due to my reputation at school I couldn't date. If anyone was interested in me, we would have a fling and kept it on the lay-low. Probably the most significant thing that happened that year was during Christmas break. Just before the break, I ran into a guy who had graduated the year before and was home on leave from the Navy. Dave was a nice guy, one of the few that would talk to me, and hold a real conversation with me. There was a Christmas dance scheduled during the break and he invited me to go. I said yes. It was the first time anyone had ever asked me to a dance. He had been going steady with a girl that graduated with him so I asked about her. He said they broke up and weren't seeing each other. When I told my parents he had asked me to the dance, my father said he wanted to meet him before I was allowed out of the house. I asked myself why? Why now? Why are you concerned about me? My mother took me shopping for a dress. Aside from our Easter outfits when we were younger, it was the only time she did that.

The magic night arrived. I did my hair, put on my dress and was all set to go. Dave was supposed to arrive early enough to meet my father. I went downstairs and waited, and waited, and waited. Two hours went by. My father said, "He stood you up." I was all set to go back to my room when a knock came at the door. Dave came in; he gave some credible excuse why he was late. I don't remember what it was. He talked with my father for a while about the Navy and we left for the dance. By the time we arrived, there were only a few stragglers hanging around. He asked if I wanted to go parking. We parked on a local dirt road not too far from my house. He opened a bottle of Jack and we sipped from it. I asked why he was late. He said that he was with his ex talking things over. They were trying to reconcile. We drank some more and made out. My coyote had transformed yet again.

Since the sixth grade a friend of mine, Crystal, would spend every weekend at my house no matter what, especially during ski season. Crystal was by my side for most of my endeavors. This was good for me because I could hide in my room all weekend with her and avoid my parents! But she almost never skied. She would sit and watch our belongings while the rest of us hit the slopes. We had a special group that went out every weekend. The only group I was accepted into was a group that, believe it or not, consisted of nerdy dope heads.

On the slopes we partied hard. We held contests like jumping moguls, racing with four or five of us attached one behind the other in groups of three or more. From the top, we would race to the bottom to see who could get there first without crashing. I was always a leader and we usually won or came in second. One time we didn't fare so well; it took the ski patrol a good half hour to pry our skis and bindings apart. We were laughing so hard, no one could move. Once in a while we wondered off the trails into the woods and got lost for hours trying to get back to the lodge.

Every summer there was a bluegrass festival that took place on the property just behind our house. The owner lent it out to the sponsors. It became so popular, Crystal and I would pitch a tent out in the backyard so that at night we could walk up to the festival and party all night, then crash all day. My father caught on after the second year and busted us. This festival was so big the news stations would cover it.

One hilarious thing that happened that summer was when my mother took me to my first rock concert. I wanted to see Blue Oyster Cult because at the time, Godzilla was huge. We were able to snag seats right in front of the stage. Halfway through the concert my mother started pulling on my leg (I was standing on a chair), yelling at me. I stepped down to hear what she was yelling about. She had caught a contact buzz from all the pot smoke. Her leg was bouncing uncontrollably and she was holding it down to get it to stop. She wanted to leave, but they had not played Godzilla yet. I told her to wait until after that song. Years later it happened again when I took her to see George Thorogood.

Summer came and the partying intensified. Rob, the daredevil, had moved into a house not far from mine. We lived out in the country where you had to walk or bike to do anything unless you were old enough to drive. One night Rob took a group of us to the local town bar. I didn't think I would get served because I was obviously underage but apparently the guys didn't think so. The bartender took an instant liking to me. Rob went to the bar to buy a round for us. When he returned, he said the bartender wanted to meet me back at Rob's house after the bar closed. We stayed for another round then headed to Rob's place. The bartender was a few cars behind on his motorcycle. Rob had invited other people from the bar so there were cars following as well. When we arrived, I went inside. I couldn't have been in there for more than five minutes when Rob and a few others came running in yelling for someone to call the cops and ambulance. I ran out the door and up the hill to the road and lying there in the middle of the road was the bartender. While backing his motorcycle up to park, one of the cars following him was speeding and didn't see him. He was hit from behind and sent flying. He lay there in pieces; his leg was ripped to shreds. He was looking at me gasping for breath. I leaned over to hold his hand while we waited for the ambulance. Someone brought a blanket to cover him. I was sooo scared, I was shaking.

When we heard the sirens, Rob yelled for me to get into the house. I left the bartender lying there; as I walked away, he gave me this long sad look. The police came, Rob did all the talking. The police officer made his way down to the house to see what was going on. I was always mistaken for someone much older, so he just looked at me and continued his questioning. By the time the ambulance and police left, it was three in the morning. Rob asked if I wanted to go for a ride since he needed to relax. We got on his motorcycle and took off. He went crazy! We went around a curve so low to the ground that I lost my shoe. We stopped at a friend's house, smoked bongs, and drank the rest of the night. He woke me up as daylight was coming through the window. I immediately panicked because I had to be home before it was discovered that I was gone. He dropped me off just shy of the hill before my house and I walked home. As I walked up the stairs, my mother was walking down. She asked what I was doing, I said I couldn't sleep. I went to bed and slept the rest of the day.

In addition to all the internal injuries the bartender had, he was laid up for weeks in the hospital. His leg was broken in three places. The doctors had to pin it together before it could even be set in a cast. He was asking for me, but I couldn't bring myself to see the guy. I didn't know him and felt uncomfortable. Why would I encourage him? Several months later, I ran into him at another bar. His leg was still in a cast. I felt bad for not going to see him so I sat and talked for a while. I even sat on his lap at his request to make him happy. He asked if we could go out. I blew him off by suggesting he recover first. I never spoke to him again.

The summer did not end without one more disturbing episode, one in which I was told never to talk about again to anyone. One night I had a dream about my neighbor's older sister, Sue. I can't explain why as I didn't know her all that well. She had to be at least 30 years old. In the dream, Sue, and her husband, Al, were driving home late at night in their car; it hit the side of an old bridge on one of the back roads. In the dream I was watching from the backseat, hovering above. I saw the car hit and catch on fire. Sue screamed as the flames were coming through the dashboard. She was trying to get out but the car was engulfed in fire. I think it was her screaming that woke me but I could feel the heat as well. It scared the living crap out of me. My heart was pounding. I looked at the clock and noticed the time. I lay awake for quite a while after that.

The next day in town, I ran into the small Mom and Pop store that Sue and Al owned. Al was in the back at the meat counter as I was walking down the middle aisle. He came around the counter and stood there staring; I was at the opposite end. It was just like my run-in with the coyote. We stood and looked at each other. I had a strange feeling but I had forgotten about the dream at that moment because I was caught up in looking at him. It was odd because I did not know the man personally.

The next morning, a Sunday, the phone rang at nine. I picked it up and it was Sue's mother. She was crying and could barely say that Sue and Al were killed earlier that morning. Their car had hit a bridge and they were burned alive! I asked her what time it happened and it was the same time I had woken from the dream the night before! I freaked out and dropped the phone. I stood in the kitchen, I couldn't move. My mother grabbed the phone and talked to her. After she hung up, I told my parents about the dream. I told them everything I saw. My father told me to never mention it to anyone. I was more than shaken by it. I was afraid to dream!

I started my sophomore year even more isolated than before. I had spent the summer with people ten years my senior. People had died - I had witnessed it and couldn't do anything to stop it. The kids I went to school with seemed immature and I was out of step with them. I wasn't into the teen drama; I had surpassed that. I manage to squeak out another year of good grades.

By the time summer rolled around, Rob's parties were out of control. Another problem had presented itself as well.

I was getting obscene phone calls; someone was stalking me. It started in the spring and continued throughout the summer. A male would call and ask all sorts of sexually explicit questions. At first I thought it was a joke from one of the idiots I went to school with. I would quiz him to see if I could tell who it was, but I could never identify the voice.

One night late in the summer just after the local fair but before the start of school, my cousin, Faith, who was visiting from California, and I were getting ready for bed when I looked out my window and spotted someone standing there. I stuck my head out the window and there he was staring up at me, but he was too far for me to recognize him. I yelled at him. My father heard me from his bedroom and asked what was going on. I told him there was a guy out in the front yard watching Faith and I change. He got up out of bed, grabbed his shotgun, opened his window, and fired a warning shot. The guy ran. He had parked his car down the hill and as he stepped on the gas, the car took off like a bat out of hell. You could hear the tires screeching all the way down the road.

My junior year proved to be more challenging. I was partying harder than ever before and the men were out of control. I always kept it quiet though. I never would kiss and tell. Hell, that is what my mother taught me and that's why the guys liked me so much. I was exactly like them. They got what they wanted and unless they bragged, no one was the wiser. By spring semester I was out of control. I was already up to my elbows in parties at Rob's, jumping from one guy to the next with no commitment. I liked it that way, no emotional attachment. What better way to avoid feelings than to keep moving like a shark, which I did. Talk about adaptability.

One night a group of us were at a bonfire and a schoolmate introduced me to his cousin, Seth, who had just moved to town. The party got out of hand, not atypical for our group and I piled into a truck with Seth and a few others to leave the party early. I was in the cab with my schoolmate who was driving, and Seth. We were going down a dirt road that came to an abrupt stop at the end of a very short hill. My schoolmate missed the stop and kept going swerving just as we were about to hit the drop off on the other side of the road. The truck veered so hard, it turned over on one side as we spun around. I instinctively grabbed for whatever was closest and that happened to be Seth's leg.

Thank God my friend straightened the truck out and got it back on the road. He drove me home. Later that night I received a phone call from Seth. He wanted to know if I was interested in him. NO not really, I was just grabbing whatever was nearby, but he turned it into something else. Talk about coyotes, he was one of the worst! This guy was a total con-artist, a real Trickster. He pushed his way into my life even though I didn't really like him. He was manipulative and controlling, but somehow he talked me into going out with him. After that, he monopolized all of my time! I was still in school trying to keep up with my grades, but that was getting harder to do with him around. Every free moment I had, he was there. My father hated him.

After a month I tried to break it off, but Seth wouldn't let me. My grades continued to drop. He was a heavy drug user and very demanding of my time. I barely made it through my finals. My father decided to take a trip to see his brother in California. He wanted me to go; not my mother and not my brothers. Actually, he wanted me away from Seth. It worked, but not without complications. While we were gone,

Seth visited our house and told my brothers that he could borrow my guitar, records and stereo, which wasn't true at all. He ended up stealing a lot of my stuff and they let him.

The trip was the best thing to ever happen to me. I felt liberated. Traveling the countryside meant freedom, although I did feel uncomfortable alone all that time with my father, staying in hotels as we made our way across the country. But I had always felt uncomfortable around him; he would do things like tickle me in inappropriate places, hide in my closet while I was undressing and wait until I was in bed with the lights out and slowly open the closet door to scare the crap out of me. I don't know why I never put the two together. I was blocking then just as I am now. I still can't put his face to the crimes that happened to me

I spent a whole month with Faith, my cousin. She is a year younger than me and we had one hell of a time. My Aunt and Uncle lived near an amusement park where we spent the whole Fourth of July weekend. While on one of the rides, we met a family of three brothers. The oldest was two years older than me. What an absolute doll! He had curly hair and blue eyes and had a great sense of humor. He reminded me of Parker Stevenson; seriously, he looked just like him and he was so irresistible I couldn't help myself. He flirted with me by splashing me from behind on a water ride. The second oldest brother was a cute blonde; Faith took a liking to him. The youngest brother was adorable too but he was the third wheel. We spent the rest of the day wandering around the park with the three boys. We went on rides, and ate junk food. It was the best time, and it was free of alcohol and drugs. We made plans to meet at a local beach for a barbecue and party the next night.

Ooh did we get into so much trouble. I managed to get both Faith and me grounded because we didn't get home by curfew. That was because I buried my father's truck in sand up to the axle at the beach and had to wait for someone to tow us out. I had never been grounded before. I pretty much did whatever I wanted because I had all the control at home. It was a new concept for me, indeed.

Back in Albany it didn't take long for me to gravitate back to the party scene. I met this guy from another town, who looked a lot like Robert Plant with the same curly blond locks, but he was just another coyote. We dated for a while. The Robert Plant dude was a heavy partier and into stuff I had not done before. Since I was generally willing to try most things at least once, I experimented with him. It didn't last long. At the same time a new bar had opened in town so I went to check it out with friends. There I ran into some guys that I went to school with. They were a year younger; one of them used to be best friends with my brother Jeff. I had known him since we were kids.

My senior year was underway and I was trying to reel in my partying ways. It didn't last very long. I started to spend more time with Rob's sister Diane and her new boyfriend. I would be totally derelict if I didn't mention Crystal, who was almost always by my side. By our senior year, she was accompanying me more and more to those nasty parties at Rob's. We are still good friends to this day because we know too much about each other. Do you really think I would give it ALL away in a book? We would do anything for each other.

I had rejoined the party crowd while trying to remain in all the upper-level classes. There were a handful of us that were together like the ski group. I had more than enough credits to graduate and couldn't see sticking around for the second semester, so I decided to graduate in January. I made plans to move back to Faith's house in California, establish residency and go to college there. As the school year got under way, the group from the bar became closer. I was seeing my Robert Plant friend intermittently and spending time with Eric, who was the friend of my brother Jeff. I kept the Robert Plant guy around just because. The funniest situation to come from that shuffle was when I inadvertently invited both my Robert Plant friend and Eric to Thanksgiving dinner. My grandparents were there too when both guys showed up. It made for an interesting dinner, that's for sure. After that, I never saw Robert Plant again.

In my senior year, the coyote was still in control, tricking me every step of the way. Thanks to my mother's teachings, I didn't find any of this out of line. I did what I was taught to do. I wasn't learning how to navigate my life at all. I didn't even know how to look for warning signs with men. I was not prepared to go out into the big bad world at all! I was really naïve.

Eric and I finally got together at a private party. That was the first night I took acid. It was quite interesting to say the least. After that we were an item at school. All those years with those ingrates and it took until my senior year before I was accepted. I was COOL! All those years when most of them wanted to beat me up, and now I was COOL? My relationship with Eric became my first real relationship, one I actually worked at. We were inseparable in a good way. Don't get me wrong; I was still drinking, using drugs, but it was the first time I had a serious relationship. All things considered, it was good. He was a very tender lover; it was my first experience with someone like that. It felt great! For the first time I was experiencing sex on another level.

The parties continued and grew increasingly more intense. The crowd I hung with was using more than alcohol and pot. They had graduated into things like acid, cocaine, mushrooms and more. I had very bad reactions to these and didn't care for them. Despite all that, we remained the 'cool' group at school.

My relationship with Eric had grown as well. We were never apart but as January neared there were obvious tensions. He wanted to get married right out of school and have kids. I wanted anything but that. California was calling me. I wanted FREEDOM! There was NO way I was going to stick around, especially if it meant staying at home. I left at the end of January; the taste for freedom was stronger than succumbing to a life in a small town, getting married and knocked up!

Chapter 3

PART ONE

This stage of the coyotes' life is where they disperse. Typically a dispersed coyote leaves the den by fall (eight months old). A dispersed coyote can become a nomad (solitary resident) - some become permanent nomads or meet up with a dispersed coyote of the opposite sex to eventually become alpha pairs of their own pack. (Grady, 32)

I left for California with Shelly, my friend from eighth grade, on a blustery cold January morning. Leaving the den wasn't hard to do, but leaving Eric was. I also felt guilty leaving my brothers with our parents. I was their protection most of the time and served as a go-between for them and my parents. At the same time, I was tired of being the parent. I had control of almost all aspects of our family. I wanted my brothers to start fending for themselves. Initially my goal for California was to get a job, work for a year, and then start school.

We were five or six hours into the trip when we blew a tire on interstate 81 in Pennsylvania. Luckily, Shelly was driving because we were traveling in the far left lane at 70 mph and had to cross over to the right during rush hour. I say luckily because Shelly had experience driving horse trailers so she was better equipped to handle the car, which was completely packed including my skis, which were strapped to the roof. We had to take everything out of the trunk just to get to the spare tire. Suitcases, boxes and bags were lined up along the side of the road as cars sped past us. The lug nuts were slightly rusted so we stood on each side of the tire iron and took turns jumping on the iron to loosen the nuts while laughing the entire time. Once we replaced the wheel and repacked the car, we headed towards Arkansas where we were staying with Shelly's cousin.

We arrived late and I was exhausted. Shelly and her cousin took the car to a shop, bought a new tire, and had it put on the car. I slept the whole night. I didn't even eat dinner. Shelly, however, went to a bar where they stayed until closing. When I woke the next morning she had had only a couple of hours of sleep, but we were back on the road by 9 am. I asked her how the hell she was able to stay up so late. She wasn't bothered since she was used to traveling the rodeo circuit. On the other hand, I required a minimum of eight hours sleep or I would automatically get sick.

The trip went fairly smoothly until we hit Arizona. There at a rest stop we ran into two guys driving a brand new Trans Am like Smokey and The Bandit. Shelly struck up a conversation with them. One of the guys was wearing a cowboy hat and she took an instant liking to him and the car. After talking with them for a while, we went into the diner to eat lunch and they joined us. As we left, Shelly asked if I would mind having the one guy ride with me in my car while she rode with the cowboy. I freaked out. She wanted a chance to drive the Trans Am and the cowboy agreed. I didn't feel right about the situation because we didn't know them, but agreed that if I wanted to stop for any reason, she had to.

We were off. Shelly hit the highway like she was racing the Indy 500! As a teenager I had always wanted to be a race car driver as my first choice, architect being my second choice. Joe watched the 500 every year so I became a fan. Naturally, Mario Andretti was my man but when Janet Guthrie made the circuit, she broke the barrier for women drivers and I lost interest.

But I had all I could do to keep up with Shelly. As we raced across Arizona I struck up a conversation with the guy next to me. I slowly learned that the cowboy had no idea who this guy was and had picked him up hitchhiking. I couldn't believe it. All sorts of things were running through my head, although he hadn't done anything weird. I immediately flagged down the Trans Am. We pulled over and I told Shelly, but she begged me to let her stay with the cowboy until we reached Los Angeles. I reluctantly agreed with yet another stipulation that when we arrived, we would get off at the first exit to switch cars. When I saw the sign for Los Angeles city limits, I flagged down the Trans Am and we exited the nearest off ramp to switch cars. When Shelly was back in the car and we were on our way, I yelled at her for ten minutes straight. She just laughed. It was all fine and good for her, as she got to drive a brand new Trans Am but I rode with a hitchhiker who no one knew anything about. How scary was that?

Years later, when *Thelma and Louise* came out, I thought about how differently it could have turned out for us. Given our past experiences with men, we could have had similar results. To this day I am very thankful that our antics didn't boomerang.

Once we arrived in California, things only got worse. Shelly had a friend from the rodeo circuit who lived in San Diego. So after arriving and spending some time with my relatives, we hit the road to visit him. It turned out that her friend had been in a terrible car crash that left him paralyzed from the waist down. He lived with his aunt and two pit bulls. We stayed the night and because he needed sex so bad, Shelly decided to help him out.

Faith and I had another cousin, Michael, that lived in San Diego and I wanted to see him. I had briefly met him when I was visiting with Joe the previous summer. Michael had lived out of the country until he was 17. He was God's gift to women and he knew it. Our physical characteristics were very similar—all three of us were Nordic type blondes. Faith and I arrived at his apartment to spend the night. This was the first time I was up close and personal with Michael. It didn't take long to find out that he was into cocaine and sex—lots of it. He talked about his exploits around the globe and with a number of our cousins too. He was a blond Michael Hutchence (of INXS fame); he exuded sex! The three of us spent an interesting evening together to say the least…

The next morning we picked up Shelly and headed back. Shelly stayed a few more days in Los Angeles, and then flew home. I was officially in Los Angeles and had to start looking for work. The problem was I had never actually worked outside of the home so I had zero experience. I wasn't interested in waitressing like Faith, so I geared my search towards a desk job in an office. While searching, I worked part time at the local convention center working events. I eventually found a job at a call center, which I hated.

It didn't take long to find trouble either! I was an 18-year-old girl from a small town who found herself in a very big city with a whole different culture and the only training I had to prepare me was what Joe and Colleen taught me, which of course wasn't the kind of preparation one's parents should give before leaving home to go to school. I was lost with no sense of direction. The group I hooked up with happened to be a band that worked at the call center during the day. At night, we would all go to a recording studio. The lead singer was the typical sexy front man (think a Billy Squier-type) and hit on me my second day on the job. Being a total groupie because I didn't know any better, I couldn't help myself. Guys in rock bands are notorious for throwing women away after having their way with them; they have to feed their egos. But, I did it anyway. The practice sessions in the studio were awful. The band spent more time arguing than actually producing music. The guys would do drugs, get loaded, argue and then inevitably go off with one of the girls that hung out in the studio. Every night it was the same thing.

One of the managers of the call center, Steve, and his partner, Jerry advised me to stay away from the band. I understood why but I was 18! Steve flirted with me as well and eventually asked me out. I didn't get a good vibe from him or Jerry. Jerry happened to be dating a woman at the call center. Eventually I relented, but asked that we double with Jerry and his girlfriend. That night I drove to their hotel to meet them. That was the weird thing about them—they lived in one hotel room together, all three of them. I walked up to the door and right away I had a bad feeling. Steve opened the door and I went in. They had pulled out some acid and asked if I wanted to join them. I hadn't touched it since my last experience because I didn't like it, but after a few drinks I gave in. We hung out for a little while, and then went to an amusement park. I felt self-conscious when we were there. Like the imaginary sign on my forehead for abuse, I felt everyone knew or could see that we were tripping. I didn't enjoy the experience—at all. In fact, it was awful. Steve and Jerry reminded me of Seth. Deep down I knew they were con-men. They and the band were nomad coyotes looking to mark their territories. I managed to avoid being drawn into the pack with the exception of my short escapade with the lead singer, who true to form, had moved on to his next victim after a few weeks.

The next day I quit the call center. The only job I had managed to find up to that point was the part time one at the convention center. That wasn't all bad. I worked several concerts, one was Rod Stewart and I also worked the Grand Prix. I loved driving to work while they were setting up the roads. They built walls and lanes and I would drive the course to see how fast I could go. It reminded me of the many times with Rob in his car or on his motorcycle.

Eric from home came to visit during a school break. He told me how everyone missed me, especially my brothers, and how much everyone wanted me to move back. I was feeling the pull but not ready to give in yet. I gave him the presidential tour of the area and introduced him to the "band" that I was still periodically hanging with. He didn't like them at all. When he returned home, he told my father that all was not well in paradise. He described the band and my heavy partying in hopes of pushing my father into doing something. At the same time, I was having my own doubts. The culture shock was overwhelming. The fact that I had no sense of what I was going to do didn't help either. Six months into my move, I decided it was time to go home. I was so confused; I thought it was best to be confused there. My father missed me but my mother who was always self-absorbed wasn't bothered by my absence. In fact, it gave her more freedom to be with her lover because I wasn't a threat.

Dad flew out to Los Angeles to drive back with me. Since we had already done the trip before, having taken two different routes there and back to see as much of the country as possible, we chose yet another route to drive back, hitting as many of the northern states as possible. That was the plan, anyway.

The trip started off okay, but then we started to talk about home and he opened up about his feelings which he had never done before. He wasn't remorseful or apologetic for all that he had done either. He was talking like a human being with feelings though. And I actually felt sorry for him; I always had and I'm not sure why. He talked about mom and the boys, and I started to feel guilty about the secrets my mother, brothers and I had kept all those years.

My father had quit drinking when I was 10 and always seemed so lonely. By high school my mother had a new boyfriend, Sam. He happened to be her boss. He would show up at the house with the excuse that he was out for a Sunday drive. Everyone knew what was going on except my father. They would chat over an elaborate breakfast my mother whipped up. It always amazed me how flawlessly she would pull it off. The lies and deceit were astounding. And my father actually liked Sam, which was unbelievable because he didn't like anyone. But to be a part of that takes its toll. Which camp should I belong to? Neither parent was a model of decent behavior but I preferred my father over my mother any day. Even after all the abuse, he didn't lie and deceive. With my mother, there was no way of knowing what was truth or fiction. Neither parent was nurturing in any way either. It was a tough call, but I would almost always side with my father. On occasion, I felt a tug in my mother's direction because my father wasn't a good husband. He never did anything special for her on birthdays like flowers or dinners. So when I was in high school, I would host birthday parties for her, doing all the planning, cooking, and invites.

As we drove home, the conversations continued. Eventually we talked about mom's affair. The thing was my father never suspected; he liked Sam and thought it was a genuine friendship. I let the cat out of the bag and finding out was a terrible shock to my father. He didn't like many people to begin with and to find out that Sam was actually carrying on an affair with his wife made him face reality big time, and it wasn't pretty.

We were two days into the trip at this point and dusk was beginning to set in so we stopped for dinner and a hotel room. We always got a room with two double beds. So, we ate and checked in. I woke up in the middle of the night with my father trying to sexually attack me. He was grabbing me and whispering in my ear that it was my mother's fault because she wouldn't have anything to do with him. He told me to punch him, do anything to stop him, which I did. I fought him off and ran to the bathroom where I locked myself in. This time he didn't knock the door down. I waited for a while to see if he would try and when he didn't, I climbed into the shower to wash myself off.

Writing about this now brings tears to my eyes. I feel sick to my stomach by the flood of feelings only other victims would know or understand. The coyote was after me in so many ways and I didn't even see it coming. This plays into the theory that once a victim, the chance of being victimized again increases exponentially. I think it is because we don't recognize when we are in a situation where we are vulnerable. Someone who grew up in a home where one was always vulnerable would be hard pressed to distinguish between a good situation and one in which they are at risk since the risk is ever present. And coyotes know this. In fact, many of them seek exactly that. They are opportunistic predators and who better to seek than one who is vulnerable and doesn't even know it.

This time I was eighteen, not four, and I couldn't erase what had happened no matter what. I blocked out the face of my abuser when I was young, but now that wasn't possible. It was and is engrained in my memory forever. After this, you would think it would have clicked that it was him all along, but I'm still not convinced, or as it has been suggested, maybe it was both men all along because there is something about that other man that lived with us that I still can't shake.

After my shower, I dressed and my father was already packed and waiting for me when I opened the bathroom door. No words were spoken; we left the hotel in the middle of the night and other than stopping for gas and food, we drove straight home.

Chapter 3

PART 2

I'm still in the dispersed stage of the coyote cycle. It can also be noted that coyotes may not form packs at all. "Depending on the area, they can live as mated pairs and bear pups that disperse when they are twelve months old." (Grady, 32)

We drove three days straight after the hotel incident. Upon arriving home, my father exited the car without saying a word and crashed on the sofa. Though I should have gone straight to bed, I immediately called Eric to let him know I was home. He was there within the hour. As we were standing outside, I told him about what happened. He went crazy, then headed towards the house—to do what, I don't think even he knew. I stopped him and said that I would deal with it, which of course I didn't. I never confronted my father about the attack, ever. I had become a pro at compartmentalizing, so that's what I did. It was how I always survived throughout the years. It was the only way I knew how to forge ahead.

Eric and I met up with our friends who wanted to hear all about my adventures. Meanwhile, Dad confronted Mom about her affair and all hell broke loose. He kicked her out of the house and once again she found herself at her sister's doorstep. When I got home later that night, he told me he had kicked her out. I didn't say anything. A few days later, my mother asked that I meet with her to talk about what happened - we met at a bar.

    She wanted to know why I ratted her out. In her opinion, everything was running smoothly. She had her lover and dad. It was all good, right? I tried to explain what happened but she didn't want to hear it. She wanted to come back home but dad set draconian conditions in which she could move back, so there was no way she would agree. I never learned what those were, but knowing my father, I imagined the worst. I suppose I deserved to be caught in the middle but I wasn't taking the blame for her actions. She was the one having the affair. I asked her why she stayed in a marriage she spent most of the time trying to escape?! She blamed her brothers and sister. She had tried to leave after Jeff was born, but they convinced her she had to stay because of us. So she did it for the financial stability, but exited the marriage emotionally almost from the beginning. No ah-ha moment there.

    After a few weeks went by, she eventually moved back into the house. The situation became unbearable. My father lived in their old bedroom and she was in with Jeff and Bill. My room was too small and I would never allow her to sleep with me. Neither parent spoke to each other unless they were arguing. My father's shift was different from hers; I think he did that on purpose to avoid her. That went on for almost a year.

    Eric and I were having our own problems. I was still looking for a job, which was difficult because I had very little experience and we were back to our old partying ways. I registered at the local community college and took a few classes. I moved in with Eric and his parents. Eric was apprenticing in construction and I eventually found a part time job at the local paper working the second shift.

A year had passed when Dad finally moved out. It was the same year Jeff was graduating from high school. I planned a big party for him and invited the whole family. My mother bought the house from my father as part of the divorce settlement, which still wasn't finalized. But all was going well. My mother had invited her boyfriend, Sam. My father showed up a few hours later. He refused to get out of his truck and asked Jeff to come out to the truck to see him. We were standing on the side of the road talking to Dad and he seemed okay. He talked to Jeff and handed him a gift, which was a very expensive diving watch. Jeff wanted to be a marine biologist. While we were talking, he hit the gas and drove into Sam's car.

Everyone heard the crash and came running because they thought something had happened to one of the kids who were playing out front. We stood in the middle of the road with our mouths wide open. Dad crushed the whole driver's side of Sam's car and damaged the entire passenger side of his truck. I felt so bad for Jeff because he could never catch a break. Everyone was in shock! Naturally, Sam was hysterical. He jumped into his car and drove off with the front fender hanging. The kicker was it was a company car and he was at our house on the weekend. Still married himself, he also had to explain it to his wife, and put a claim into the company. Actually there is a sort of karma in that. Shortly after his car was crushed, his houseboat was also broken into while docked. Someone had completely trashed it. Geez, I wonder who was responsible?

Needless to say, we didn't see Sam for a while. My mother was asked to leave her job. Sam knew quite a few business owners and found her a position nearby. Their relationship continued for a while longer until he retired. His wife wanted to move south to the Carolinas, which they did. There was some drama when he decided he wanted to be with my mother instead. She flew down to drive back with him; they made it half way home when he changed his mind. He went back to his wife. It didn't take long for my mother to hook up with another guy, Jim, who worked at the new company. He happened to be married as well. Is it just me or do you see a pattern here?

I had moved back home and was working part time. Eric and I were still having problems and to fix them, we agreed to watch his grandparents' house for the summer while they were away at camp. By that time, I had finally landed a full time accounting job in the city. A little more than a year had passed since the drive home with my father and we still weren't speaking. My relationship with my mother was strained as well. So, agreeing to watch their house for the summer was a no-brainer.

The first few weeks went well, but midway through the summer, cracks were developing between us, and our relationship was showing obvious signs of strain. Eric wasn't coming home from work right away and I was spending more time with a friend from work, Barb, who lived in the next town over with her boyfriend. They were more my league according to Eric. Part of the strain was that he was a slob. The longer we were together, the more I realized that was going to be my life if I stayed with him. It would be one thing if he was sloppy and all I had to do is ask him to pick up, but he wasn't bothered by dirt and grime and broken crap lying around both inside and outside. It drove me nuts! Plus, he didn't like my new friends because they were too elite. His problem with me was I wouldn't marry him and have babies!

The tension between us was growing. Additionally, I was having problems with allergies so my doctor referred me to an allergist who wanted to do some testing. I took an afternoon off from work to have the tests. Eric's grandparents were home that particular week so I went back to my mother's. I was totally out of whack from all the shots. Regardless, I decided to visit a cousin of mine and her husband. I drove into town to get gas and noticed Eric's truck there, but didn't see him. I filled up and headed towards my cousin's. I stayed for a few hours then went home. When I arrived, Eric was there waiting for me. He asked where I had been and I told him I went to visit my cousin. He said I was lying, that he saw me drive out of town in the opposite direction towards the gas station. I told him I filled up my car, turned around and drove to my cousin's. He insisted I was lying. He accused me of going to Rob's house, who happened to live on that side of town. I told him that was ridiculous. I was totally baffled by the argument. He was never one to yell at all, so to yell at me about something so ridiculous was very strange and out of character.

That Friday I found out why. Eric met up with me at my mother's house after work and told me he wanted to break up. He said it wasn't working out. That caught me completely off guard. Looking back on it, all the warning signs were there. I asked if we could work at the relationship and he said no. I was upset and asked if we could at least talk about it. He stayed through the night. In the morning he revealed that he was seeing someone else. I found out a few days later that it was a high school junior and she was pregnant—just what he wanted!

After the breakup, I went wild! I was hanging out in the bars almost every night. On Fridays I would hit happy hour at the local Marriott. For me it would turn into an all-nighter. I was also hanging out with Rob and his friends again. We weren't dating but would hook up periodically. My drinking was out of control as well. A new family had bought the local bar in town and their son typically bartended. He was into all sorts of extracurricular activities. The bar became the local hangout for a chosen few after hours. Rob would show up just before closing and order pitchers of kamikazes, then line up shot glasses. Having had a few Jack Daniels and ginger ales by then, he would insist that I do a shot with him. We had our usual seats at one end of the bar. When the bar closed and the last of the patrons left, the bartender would wipe down the bar and Rob and a few others would bring out bags of coke and do lines. I stayed away from it for the most part. Some nights I would get home just in time to shower and leave for work.

One night, Rob and I were sitting at the bar having pitchers of kamikazes when a fight broke out. The guys piled on top of each other—hands, fists and feet were flying. Rob pushed me towards the wall to get me out of the way as they made their way towards us. I was trapped as the whole group just kind of fell on us. My legs were pinned to the bar. At the same time someone's fist came up out of the pile and hit me square in the face. The whole pile fell over on the floor and Rob and a few others broke it up and escorted the lot of them outside.

On a separate occasion, I was in the bar when another group of guys came in. They were raucous. It didn't take long before a fight broke out, only this time someone drew a knife! That night the woman bartender and I were watching as these guys were threatening to kill each other and then the guy with the knife threw it. It flew passed its intended target and headed right for us. We both ducked just in time! It stuck in the wall behind my head. The bartender called the police. We were there for quite a while answering questions and describing what happened. They arrested the guy with the knife.

I began to spend a lot more time with a friend, Barb, from work. I had moved up in my position at the distributor of mechanical products where I worked and was recently put in charge of the main warehouse in addition to three of the largest branches. I did all the accounts payable for all four locations but my biggest responsibility was the main warehouse.

Barb and I would go to the Marriott for happy hour on Fridays. One night at the Marriott a group of people next to us were having a conversation; Barb became interested in what they were saying and joined in their conversation. She liked one of the guys, but since she was already involved, she suggested I start talking to him. I looked over her shoulder and there was this older petite man, who was not a hell of a lot taller than me and about the same size, with dark hair and a very nice tan even though it was late November. He was dressed in a suit and looked very handsome indeed.

My head told me that this guy would never be interested in me because I was a loser, but Barb kept prodding me to talk to him. His name was Ray; he seemed okay, and nothing really struck me as odd. After a few more drinks, he asked if I wanted to go slumming. Slumming? What was that? I wasn't familiar with this term at least in the sense that he meant it, which was to dress down and hit the local town bars. I didn't think it was a good idea to tell him that I hung at my local town bar. Apparently, according to his definition, I was slumming all along and didn't know it. I told him I would have to drive home to change because I was still in my work clothes and by time I did that, it would be too late. He suggested I go back to his place and he would dress me in his clothes and we could go from there. I looked at Barb giving her the cross-eyed look. I pulled her off to the side and said no way. She thought he could be trusted. She had a good feeling about him. But my skepticism said to be wary.

We drove back to his place, a guest house, behind one of the mansions located at the top of one of the largest hills in the city. It had a bird's eye view of the surrounding area. My curiosity was piqued. We entered the guest house through the side entrance, which is where he kept his wood for the fireplace. The kitchen was a typical '50s kitchen with an old Chambers cook stove. As we made our way through the kitchen into the living area, I took in the smell of the kitchen where he actually had a pot of soup warming. The living area had exposed beams and one of the largest stone fireplaces I had ever seen. I could actually stand in it. The embers from a fire that had just died out were still warm. Ray added a few logs to it then turned to the stairs where he directed me. With much apprehension I followed. He pointed to the first bedroom saying it was his roommate's, then straight ahead to his. We entered and he walked towards his closet. He took out a pair of army fatigues and a flannel shirt, handed them to me, and said he thought they would fit and asked me to change. The bathroom was downstairs. While I was changing, he put on a similar outfit.

I stepped out of the bathroom; he was there to inspect my attire. He put a hat on my head, adjusted it, and said we were ready to go. We drove down the hill and parked. He took me to a local pub, a hole in the wall, but it was a good time. We went back to his place and sat in front of the fire. We talked a while and I fell asleep on the sofa. He covered me with a blanket. I woke the next morning to the smell of freshly brewed coffee.

As I lay there on the sofa with the events from the night before swirling around in my head, I wondered why he didn't pressure me to have sex. This was the first time I went out with a guy who didn't try to take advantage of me. I didn't know what to think. I was taught that is what you do, but Ray didn't. Funny, I thought there was something wrong with me. Was I not his type? Did he not find me attractive, smart or funny? All these thoughts went around in my head. We drank coffee beside the fire and talked. He was in the middle of a divorce and had a young son. He was in a custody battle with his wife who wouldn't let him see his son. I wondered why. What was wrong with him that his wife wouldn't let him see his son? He was soft spoken and seemed gentle. He had been injured in Vietnam.

I told him I was still reeling from my relationship with Eric mostly due to how we broke up. I stayed a bit longer then headed home. Before leaving, he asked if he could see me again. I said yes and we exchanged numbers. The experience left me with a lot of unanswered questions, but I enjoyed it. It was relaxing because he never made it about sex. Though I was taught that is what you do, I always felt extremely uncomfortable knowing I had to put out because I thought I HAD to. For once, I felt comfortable and at ease.

The holidays came and went and we were in the middle of an icy cold winter. But that didn't stop my reckless liaisons, which were starting to take a toll. In addition to my budding friendship with Ray, I had met a guy from work, Tom. Tom was recently hired for a new program that the vice president of the main warehouse initiated. We would talk periodically at the coffee machine, sometimes in the hall. He was two years my senior, a spot on petite version of Tom Selleck and a charmer. But, I didn't really give him a second thought. Besides my budding relationship with Ray, I had an on and off thing with a guy that graduated from my high school. He would come into the bar just before closing, we would have a drink together then I would follow him to his apartment in the city, but that relationship was purely platonic.

I was playing the field, and why not? It was the early '80s and that's what everyone did. Pretty much like a Carrie Bradshaw in real life. Not something I'm proud of, but it is my past and it helped to shape the person I've become.

One day at work, Barb and I were discussing how she and her husband had met. Barb had married the summer before. She explained that she was at a downtown bar one night and took an instant liking to him. She then turned to her friend and said that she was going to marry him and that, she did. I thought that was ridiculous. So jokingly, I looked over at the coffee machine and Tom happened to be standing there. I pointed to him and said okay, someday I'm going to marry him. We both laughed because Tom and I had not been out on a date. Hell, I wasn't sure if he was even interested in me. A few weeks later, Tom asked me out.

Tom and I started out at the Marriott happy hour. After a few rounds, he suggested we go to another bar. We each had our own cars. When we walked out to our cars, the temperature had dropped so low that the parking lot and roads were covered with ice. We headed out anyway. I was in front of him as we were rounding a ramp to enter the main highway. It was snowing heavily and the ramp was icy. As we drove through the tolls, a car came up behind me and Tom was behind it. As we made our way around the loop, my car went into a spin and I lost control. I spun around doing a complete 360 degree turn. As I was spinning, I happened to look in my rear view mirror and saw that Tom's car was doing the same! The person (s) in the car between us must have been having a heart attack. Tom noticed that my car was spinning too. Each of us were able to pull out of it and managed to get onto the highway. A miracle indeed.

When we finally arrived at the next bar, we couldn't stop talking about what happened. I was still shaking. But we laughed, thinking how coincidental it was that we both spun out at the same time. As the evening wore on, he suggested we get a room at a local hotel, so we did. By the time we checked in, the alcohol from earlier had taken its toll, so there was not much in the way of action. We didn't stick around long the next morning either, as he wanted to go work out and I needed to head home. The following Monday at work, he ignored me. Unlike Ray, Tom was willing to take advantage of me. He victimized me afterward by ignoring me. A huge red flag I chose to ignore.

I let that go on for a little more than a week. Not willing to remain the secret partner yet again, I decided to take action. I took a huge piece of paper and wrote "you are an asshole" and put it on his windshield. Everyone at work saw it. It didn't take long for him to seek me out. He apologized but was also slightly embarrassed by his lack of performance the night we went out. He promised we would go out again, but I didn't give it much thought.

In the meantime, I was still seeing Ray. We didn't date per se; I would go to his house and hang out. We talked a lot. It wasn't a sexual relationship, but we made love a few times; he was a very tender lover. I was also dating others here and there. Occasionally, I would hook up with Rob; I couldn't resist his bad boy ways. But I was growing tired of the same routine of work, drink all night, and if I was lucky, get some sleep. I decided I needed a break from all the partying. I started to make plans with my cousin Michael who had moved to Miami. When I called Michael he said, you know you are coming down during spring break? I didn't realize it when I booked the flight.

The night before my trip, I ran into Eric at the bar and we talked. He was feeling the pressure and stress regarding his teenage girlfriend who was very much pregnant. He had heard through the grapevine that I was out and about, having a good time. He was apologetic and wished our relationship had turned out differently. I couldn't help but think that he was getting exactly what he wanted. However, I still had very strong feelings for him and was feeling the pull. He left before me and I waited a while before I called him from the bar pay phone. I told him it wasn't too late and I asked him to join me on the trip. He said no. It was his responsibility to take care of her and that was that.

I flew out late the next night, and arrived in Miami at 1:00 am. Michael fell asleep while waiting to pick me up. I had to call Michael from the airport pay phone several times to wake him up to come and get me. Once at his place, he ran through the "rules." The number one rule was to never drive the I-95 at night. The Cuban refugees from the

Mariel boat lift were living under the I-95 in tents. He said that at night they would throw Molotov cocktails up on the highway to stop cars to rob them. I didn't believe him, but I saw for myself the burned out cars still sitting on the sides of the highway. Michael stored a gun under the seat in his car for protection. He told me how the refugees would get up on cars and start shooting bullets through the roofs of cars, so he wanted to be prepared. Because of the situation in Miami, the second rule was to stay in Fort Lauderdale if I was still out at sunset. He had a friend I could stay with if that happened to be the case.

The next night, Michael took me to dinner. We went back to his apartment and smoked a joint and talked about our screwed up family. He told me things I didn't know about our grandparents—the business they owned and the fact that my grandmother was in a car accident with her lover. She was severely injured and had received a large sum of money from the settlement. Shortly after that, due to her poor money management, my grandparents lost the dairy bar they owned and my grandfather had to work for one of the local milk processing plants as a manager. I was still stunned by the affair part of the conversation when he said that my grandmother blamed my uncle (Michael's father) for the loss of the business. She told people my uncle had messed it up, when in fact it was her meddling. I sat there shaking my head. I told him how she took the money my father received from his settlement. He didn't know about my father's accident, but after telling me about the other stuff, I saw why my father had issues with his parents. I still wasn't getting the abuse part though. Michael never mentioned anything like that, although I know Michael didn't get along with his father either. It's like the whole family hated their own sons.

I lounged around Michael's apartment complex while he was at work; he worked at the yacht club at the local marina. After work, he took me to the beach where we stayed a few hours. I got sunburned beyond sunburned! I had on a crocheted French bikini so when I took it off, I had lines running up and down my boobs and butt. They looked like little mice foot prints! Michael laughed his ass off. He rubbed aloe all over me, all I could do was lay there…

The next day I went to Fort Lauderdale. Had I known what Fort Lauderdale was all about during spring break, I wouldn't have gone. The next three days were an absolute blur… I hooked up with Michael's friend so that I had a place to stay, but it's best not to go into detail here—most know about spring break, 'nuf said.

My first day back at work, I ran into Tom. He was impressed with my tan. What he couldn't see were the blisters on my chest, back and legs. I told him how badly I burned—I pulled up my shirt exposing my bra, but clearly visible were the raw burn lines around my chest. The look on his face was disbelief. He asked me out a few days later.

The following Thursday night I ran into a schoolmate, who was a truck driver, at a local bar. I was interested in him when we were in school, but he was part of a different group who were snobs. Honestly, I was shocked he was even talking to me. He talked about his experience as a truck driver. Traveling meant freedom to me so when he asked if I would be interested in riding with him, I jumped all over that. In fact, he was leaving for a trip the next night, which happened to be a Friday—so I said yes!

After work, I went home and packed a small bag. We picked up the tractor trailer, which was already loaded and ready to go. It was a standard trailer with an older cab. A couple of hours into the trip, we hit some bad weather in the mountains. Snow was blowing everywhere reducing the visibility. Trucks were ascending and descending very slowly, one behind the other in the right lane. Once we cleared the mountains we were fine. We stopped at a truck stop, ate a very late dinner and slept in the cab until daylight. My insides felt like they were a jumbled mess. The cab wasn't a luxury cab like so many you see today, so riding in it felt like being in a non-stop bounce house. The trip was fascinating to say the least; I learned a lot about the forbidden group and him, not to mention the ride in the big rig. Let's just say that I have great respect for the folks who drive trucks for a living. I never saw him after the trip, but I was okay with that.

I was still seeing Ray on and off but it was nothing serious. So as I navigated all the coyotes in my midst, Tom and I began to see more of each other. He had relocated to another branch of our company so I drove out to see him on the weekends. Summer was very busy, between work and driving to see Tom. There were weekends where Tom was busy so I stayed home and hung with whoever was around at the time.

One particular weekend while I was hanging at the bar, a friend from school walked in. I was shooting pool with his sister and he asked to join. He was very intoxicated. He had been drinking all day because his girlfriend had just broken up with him. He was going on about how his life was over; his sister and I told him to sleep it off and tried in vain to convince him that things would be better in the morning. We insisted that it would work out for the best. We shot a couple rounds of pool. He decided he had enough and wanted to head home, which was just across the parking lot. I gave him a big hug and reassured him that once he slept off the alcohol, things would look better. He left, walked across the parking lot up to his apartment and blew his brains out.

Tom and I were spending almost every weekend together so our relationship was growing, so I thought, but there were already red flags that I was choosing to ignore or simply didn't understand. It was August; one of the guys he worked with was having a housewarming party and Tom invited me. This was the first time I was introduced to some of the people we worked with from one of the branches I was put in charge of. Little did I know at the time, my attendance at the party caused a reaction in someone else and that led to one of the most public humiliating moments in my life.

It started out with incoming phone calls to Tom's apartment. I would answer and the person would hang up. One time I answered, a woman laughed and then hung up. Tom said he had no idea why someone would do that. This went on for a couple of weeks. I started having a feeling that something bad was going to happen. It reminded me of when I had the dream about my neighbor's accident. One day at work I started to get that feeling and it was growing stronger and stronger as the day went on. I told a coworker that something really bad was going to happen and that I felt like throwing-up. At first she said it was all in my head, but then her expression changed and she looked at me strangely. She motioned behind me.

There standing in the doorway was the HR assistant who supposedly had taken the day off. She asked to speak with me privately outside. She proceeded to tell me that she and Tom had been seeing each other all summer and that she was supposed to go to that housewarming party but couldn't; that was when Tom asked me. When? When were you seeing him? Some weekends he was busy, but I was there most of the time. When she found out I went with him to the party, she confronted him and he lied to her. She told him to tell me the truth about them or she would. He refused, so she took the day off to tell me. I was in shock! After she left, I vaguely remember walking up to my friend's desk. I was trembling. She said that the next time I had a bad feeling she was going to listen to me because I had a sixth sense. Between finding out about Tom and the HR chick and the embarrassment of all my coworkers witnessing it, to say I was absolutely mortified would be an understatement.

When I called Tom to ask about her, he denied the relationship. He said they had only gone out a few times and swore he didn't know what she was talking about. He convinced me to drive to his place after work to talk, so I did. I decided we should stop seeing each other, but he insisted that he wanted to keep our relationship going. I didn't believe him. Common sense says he was the one lying. No one goes to that amount of trouble in their work place, over nothing, especially not an HR employee. He begged me to stay, saying that I was the only one for him. After a weekend of his begging, I gave in, ignoring the red flag.

Not too long after that incident, Tom went to visit one of his fraternity brothers in New Jersey who had just bought a home. He flew out on Friday and was to return late Sunday night. I went to his apartment while he was gone to clean a little and hang out with some of our friends from work.

He said that wasn't necessary, but that he wasn't going to say no. Why should he—he had himself a maid.

I drove to the apartment after work and immediately started to wash the dishes which was my routine by then, and then, called a couple of people to see if they wanted to go out. I headed out to pick them up. First, was a guy that worked in the warehouse at Tom's branch. He got in the car and proceeded to tell me that he liked me a lot and couldn't sit idly by while Tom was with another woman. I parked in the nearest shopping center lot and turned to look at him. He explained how Tom made up the story about visiting his fraternity brother and that he was really staying with a girl he met in South Carolina who worked for one of our vendors. They hadn't physically met before, but his interest in her was enough that he wanted to spend the weekend with her. This guy also told me that our mutual woman friend from the office also knew about Tom's rendezvous with this girl. I was speechless. I pulled out of the parking lot and drove to our friend's house. She got in the car and I immediately confronted her with what I had just found out and she confirmed it. I was so mad I stomped on the clutch and was barreling through the city.

We arrived at the bar and our woman friend asked me to take her back home. She didn't want to be a part of anything that night. At that point, I agreed that going out was not an option. I decided to drive home. I had to stop back at the apartment to get my things. Our guy friend had other things on his mind like getting high. He asked if he could go to the apartment with me. I didn't have a problem because he was just a friend. While I packed, he took out a rather large bag of coke and started to line it. He asked if I wanted some. At first I said no because I didn't like the stuff, but then, I changed my mind. I had to drive home and it was late so maybe a little wouldn't hurt. The little turned into a lot as I sat there fuming over what was happening. By the time I left, it was early morning. I was so sick from the coke, I felt like I was going to die. But I wasn't going to stay there.

When I walked through the front door at home, my mother was standing there. She took one look at me and suggested I go to the emergency room. Now mind you, my mother never offered to take anyone to the doctor. Not when I was lying on the sofa for at least a week with an ear infection or when Jeff was hit in the head with a rock with blood gushing down his head, my parents just told him not to fall asleep. Or the time I was dragged by the horse and obviously had a concussion. So for her to suggest that I go to the emergency room tells you I was in really bad shape. I said no and made my way to my room. I didn't get up until the next morning.

What type of coyote was Tom? He was probably a shape-shifter and trickster for sure. It was highly likely he was a pathological liar as well. Additionally, a narcissistic personality is typical of the predator coyote. The narcissist doesn't think his actions affect others or doesn't care. But, I didn't connect the dots at the time.

That Monday, I stayed with Crystal because on my way home from Tom's, I snapped the clutch in my brand new car. I had to get towed back to the house, so I was without a car. Our friend told Tom that I knew where he was over the weekend. Tom eventually called Crystal's. He had called everywhere looking for me; those were the first words out of his mouth. I asked why he was calling. He said that he hadn't heard from me so he thought something was wrong.

I told him he was full of shit. He knew exactly what had happened. He wanted to talk about it, but I refused.

That Friday he drove to Crystal's apartment and stood outside yelling up at me. He was begging me to come down to talk about it. I refused, but he wouldn't stop. Crystal and her roommate couldn't stand it anymore and made me listen to what he had to say. It was more of the same. He admitted he made a mistake. When he got to South Carolina, he ended up staying on the couch which I didn't believe. Later I found out that I was right. He asked me to visit for the weekend so we could talk about it. He drove me home so I could pack.

As we drove to his apartment he said he was done with other women and wanted us to be together. At this point, the only thing running through my mind was that he was a pathological liar. I couldn't be with someone like that because it was too much like my mother. He swore that he wasn't lying and invited me to dinner at his parents' house. He was going for the weekend and wanted me to meet them. This step is usually serious and I agreed, but only because I was curious. I figured I would at least check out his family.

One evening after returning from Tom's, I stopped in at the bar closest to my house down the old dirt road. I was talking with the bartender who was a good friend. I had had a crush on him for the longest time—he looked like Bon Scott, I swear to God, but it never happened and we were just good friends. Anyway, I was sitting at the bar having a conversation with Bon when the guy from the bar fight with the knife walked in. He set his eyes on me and started to walk towards me. Ever since I gave my statement to the police, he and his brothers had it out for me. Bon told me to go home.

I was heading towards my car when the guy came up behind me, grabbed me and pulled me into his truck. He started to assault me, trying to take my clothes off. Did I mention he was loaded? I fought him off, scratching and punching; somehow I grabbed hold of the door handle and fell out of the truck. I righted myself and ran to my car, started it and drove home as fast as I could. He was in hot pursuit. I turned the corner at the end of the road barely making it and sped up the hill to the house. We had five large maple trees that lined the front yard; I pulled in between them and right up to the front steps. I ran in and yelled for my brothers to come. I was yelling that one of the Smith brothers was chasing me and he was pulling up to the house. Jeff and Bill ran out the front door just as the guy was jumping out of his truck. They headed him off and told him they would kill him if he ever laid a finger on me again. I was shaken and black and blue. A few nights after that, I stopped in to tell Bon what the asshole did and he couldn't believe it.

It was the weekend and I was going to Tom's parents for dinner. I pulled up to the house; the property of 26 acres had a huge pond on it. I was really impressed. The pond is even listed on the New York State map. Tom had gone for a jog, so I chatted with his mother and younger brother. When he walked in from his run, I looked at him. That was the moment I thought I might be able to marry this guy. I was keeping my emotions to myself especially after what he had done. I thought it could work. We had a lot in common, if we could just get past all his lies. It wasn't a horrible visit. His father was a blow-hard, a total control freak and I should have taken a cue from that. Tom isn't a blow-hard, but he is a total control freak. I met his sister and her husband; they were building a new house. She was pregnant and expecting any day. Tom is the oldest of his siblings, like me, so we had that in common too.

Back at home, I met up with Ray one last time at the guest house. We sat out on the hill over-looking the city. The view was phenomenal. I told him about Tom and that it was getting serious. We talked for a while, went to dinner and I drove him home. He wished me the best with Tom and I wished him the best with his son.

Once again the holidays were approaching. I made a deal with a friend to buy his king size waterbed for Tom. It was in excellent condition and Tom needed something other than the twin bed his parents gave him. Or more accurately, I needed something better for my back. I made arrangements with a friend of Tom's to take Tom out for the day while I moved the bed in and got it set up. The guy I bought it from agreed to help me. Everything that could have gone wrong did! But we eventually got it set up. When Tom and his friend arrived it was still filling because we were so far behind schedule, but he was surprised. After everyone left, Tom handed me a wrapped box. When I opened it, it had a note to go to another location. There was a note that said to go to yet another location and this went on for several notes, until I reached a pocket of a particular shirt in the closet and in that pocket was another box. He had bought me a pair of diamond earrings.

After the holidays, Tom was staying in the area so I took him up to the bar to introduce him around. He didn't know many of my friends because he lived in Utica. While we were there, Eric walked in. He came over to talk - - to catch up, really, but Tom wasn't having it. Tom grabbed my arm and dragged me out of the bar and we drove back to my mother's. We weren't in the door two minutes when the phone rang. I picked up and it was Eric. He asked if I was okay. He didn't like the way Tom grabbed me. Eric would never grab a woman—ever, he was a teddy bear. He was afraid Tom was hurting me. He was but it wasn't unbearable.

Tom heard Eric questioning his actions. He picked up a kitchen chair and threw it across the kitchen; it landed in the living room. The noise woke my mother. She ran down the stairs to find out what was going on. Tom stormed out of the house to go back to the bar. I quickly phoned the bar and asked for Eric. I asked him not to have it out with Tom. Eric was a big guy and could have easily done some serious damage, but I didn't want him to get in trouble. I told him to just let Tom blow off some steam but to stay away. I hung up and drove back to the bar to head Tom off. When I arrived, they were at the bar drinking beer. I walked up and Eric winked at me.

It was another red flag I chose to ignore. Tom was possessive. I was a possession to him, not an equal. But at the same time, no one had fought for me before, so I confused his actions with love. Not knowing what love was, it was easy to be confused. The coyote had exposed himself. He expressed both good and bad qualities, none of which were as bad as living with my parents. That's what I was thinking.

I moved in with Tom that March just a little more than a year after we had met. He immediately took control of my finances. My entire paycheck was deposited into his checking account and he took care of my bills. Looking back on it now, I see how stupid I was, but at the time I was glad someone was taking care of me for a change. Looking out for my best interest, so I thought; I wasn't used to that. I didn't understand that he was doing it to control me.

Initially, I was quite comfortable in our arrangement. Summer came and we hung out with Tom's fraternity brothers that would drift in for a party. We also traveled to his frat house for beer blasts. But Tom was growing tired of his job and wanted to go back to school. Instead of going for an MBA, he decided to study engineering. Getting into the particular school he wanted was another story. You had to be the best of the best so when he was finally accepted, he was overjoyed! Shortly after, he got down on one knee and proposed to me. In his words, "now that I have a future, I want you to be a part of it - will you marry me?" I said yes. We set a date for the following fall, my favorite time of the year. He started classes that fall. I was working in the media department of an advertising agency.

After the holidays, Tom received a phone call from a headhunter about a possible job and agreed to a phone interview. A few weeks later the company phoned and asked if he was interested in meeting with them. The interview was in New York City and it was first thing Monday morning, the day after the Super Bowl. So we traveled early that Sunday morning to be in the hotel in time to watch the Super Bowl. It was January 25, 1987, the Giants vs. Broncos. Tom was offered the job which meant we would have to move to the city. It was his dream job so he accepted the offer and we moved to northern New Jersey that spring.

Once settled in, I found a job with another advertising agency. At the same time, I was traveling back and forth for the wedding preparations. Right after we were engaged, I picked out a dress in Utica, but the rest of the wedding party had to shop in Albany. So I was driving between New Jersey, Utica and Albany. In August, Tom was asked to relocate to the Boston office. So we were packing our apartment in

New Jersey, traveling to Albany and Utica because of the wedding dress, and moving to Massachusetts. All of this just weeks before the wedding!

Initially I didn't want my father to be part of the wedding, but friends convinced me that I should give him the opportunity. I introduced Tom to my father in the spring when we were moving to New Jersey. Surprisingly, Dad liked Tom. I was surprised that he agreed to walk me down the aisle. I told him that he should step up and help pay for the wedding because Tom and I were paying for a lot of it ourselves. I also told him that he had to be on his best behavior because Mom's boyfriend was going to be there.

Over the years, my brother Jeff had become an alcoholic and recluse. He was incapable of communicating with the outside world. He borders on schizophrenia and is severely paranoid. I can understand the paranoia because my father was always after him. I've tried throughout the years to help him, but he needs professional help. Maybe he is beyond help. He can't be around people. Needless to say, I couldn't get him to come to our wedding.

Bill, on the other hand, was in our wedding. He was the basketball team's star in high school and his name appeared in the paper regularly. Bill is outgoing, but he is a thief, and a pathological liar like my mother. He didn't drink but loved his pot. However, there were problems with keeping him in school. Apparently, my mother wouldn't buy him shoes for basketball or new clothes. She was always like that. Everyone knew my father made good money so this was always a mystery. Anyway, I didn't find out about the basketball shoes until after the wedding. The coach felt so bad for Bill, that he went out and bought him a new pair. How embarrassing for Bill and there was NO reason for it. Our family would make a great case study. Really, what happens to three siblings when they grow up in an abusive family - suffering from sexual, emotional and physical abuse?

Once Tom and I moved to Attleboro, Massachusetts, more red flags were waving. Tom's new boss was a real snob. He took an immediate dislike to me. We moved into our condo three weeks before the wedding and Tom's boss had him out drinking almost every night or so he said. Some nights he wouldn't come home at all. In fact, the night we were to drive back to Albany for our wedding, Tom's boss took him out and tried to talk him out of marrying me. How ironic because it should have been the other way around. Tom came home late that night. I was pissed because we were supposed to be on the road by the time he rolled in drunk.

On the way to Albany, I told him I didn't want to go through with the wedding. I didn't want to live my life like the last three weeks and he obviously didn't want the marriage either. He said that wasn't true and he did want to marry me. He spent the whole trip trying to convince me. Once there, I was caught up in all the hoopla of the wedding but had expressed my concerns to my father of all people. I told him about all the late nights and drinking.

The day arrived with much trepidation. In fact, there is a photo of my father and me as we were walking down the aisle. We were smiling because under his breath he said, "Now is the time to turn and run - I won't stop you!" He made me laugh.

Chapter 4

PART 1

The Pack: Typically consists of three to eight coyotes with an average pack size of six. The pack consists of the alpha pair (mating pair) and two or more beta coyotes. The beta coyotes protect the pack and pups - they are permanent members (pups who have not dispersed by November after birth). The coyote social structure is very important as they rely on strong family bonds and shared territories for survival. (Grady, 31)

After honeymooning in the Caribbean, we returned to our condo in Massachusetts. I had taken a job in Providence, Rhode Island, with another advertising company working as the owner's secretary. I didn't like it—I'm not a secretary. Fall was in full swing and Tom was back to his usual antics. He would stay out late with his boss and "customers." Given my past experiences with him, I had my doubts that he was with "customers." We argued constantly. On top of that, the people living above us, a couple with two small children also argued. He would hit her and throw things. This was too much like home. Tom and I argued about his late nights, but at least it was nothing like the couple above us?! To make matters worse, our condo was across from a cemetery and given my past experience with death and dreams, I was extremely uncomfortable being there alone.

Thanksgiving was approaching. I had the crazy idea to invite my father and he accepted. The day before Thanksgiving, Tom drove me to work since he had the day off. In the time it took him to drive me to work and return to the condo, someone had taken a crowbar to our door and ripped through the condo, stealing Tom's entire stereo system, all my jewelry, and a fur coat my father had bought me for Christmas, a make-up gift after the incident. Everything was turned upside down! Tom called the police; once they were there, he drove back to get me because I was having a panic attack. My poor dog was found shivering under the sofa in the second bedroom. She ran and hid when they broke in. We had the police there the rest of the day, taking fingerprints, notes and an inventory of the stolen items. Tom was upset about his equipment. It was an expensive system he had bought while in college with the money he made working at a bar. My dresser drawers had been dumped on our bed. My underwear was strewn all over. This was invasion of privacy on a different level, the story of my life.

It was too late to call my father to stop him from coming. He arrived around 5:00 that evening. After finding out about what had happened, and the pure exhaustion from the day, we decided to drive to P-Town where we had dinner. Thanksgiving morning I put the turkey in and spent the day cleaning the mess the thieves and police had left.

After the theft, I had a hard time sleeping especially when Tom decided not to come home. One night in particular, I woke up so stuffed up from the forced air heating, I couldn't breathe. I ran out into the parking lot in the middle of the night in just my nightgown so I could get some fresh air. As I turned to go back into the building, I realized I forgot my key. We were in a security building (yeah, right. The neighbor two floors above us had buzzed the thieves in the day we were broken into). I stood outside pounding on the door. It was January and it was freezing. Finally, the condo next to us heard me screaming and they let me in but I was also locked out of our condo. So I sat in their place in my nightgown trying to call Tom to come home. Luckily I remembered the restaurant he said he'd be at and was able to reach him there. He thought I was joking just to get him to come home. So I had to put our neighbor on the phone to confirm I was in fact locked out and sitting there in my nightgown. What an asshole! It seemed like forever waiting for him to get there. He was in Boston. When he finally arrived, he said his boss thought I did it on purpose. Another asshole!

Not long after, Tom was asked to relocate to the northern district of Boston and the states of New Hampshire and Maine. By spring we moved into a duplex in Portsmouth, New Hampshire. Once we were settled in, Tom was back to his shenanigans. I had to look for work yet again and my track record wasn't looking good. We had moved so much in such a short time that trying to convince a prospective employer that I was a good candidate for any job was laughable. I couldn't guarantee anything and to make matters worse, Tom would grill me every night about how many jobs I had applied for and interviews I went on. It didn't seem to register in his brain that all the moving made it hard for me. It wasn't his job he was constantly giving up.

I landed an executive assistant position for a shoe manufacturer. The first few days were okay. The guy I worked for was a young man from New Jersey. He asked if I would mind working late if he needed me to. I didn't have a problem because Tom was seldom home at a decent hour. On the third day of my new job, my boss invited me to lunch. He proceeded to tell me about belonging to a porn club and asked what I thought about porn and threesomes. He mentioned that he had extra work and wondered if I would work late that night with him. BIG RED FLAG! After my experiences I knew where this was headed. When we returned to the office, I grabbed my stuff and walked out. The trickster coyote was still hounding me, tricking me into thinking I was going to be this big executive secretary, only to find out he wanted sex. I could NOT believe my luck. How was I going to explain this? So, the sign was hung on my forehead for all to see, it just wasn't visible to me when I looked in the mirror.

When Tom arrived home that night I told him I quit. He had a fit but when I told him why, he was angry. Because, as you know, no one was allowed to touch me only him, when he deemed it necessary. I was a possession. He was out having a good time most nights and I was left home. I was there to serve him. On occasion, Tom would invite me to attend some of the dinners and I would drive to a park and ride just over the Massachusetts border. He would pick me up and drive to Boston. We had some good times in Boston and did a lot of fine dining, but I was always suspicious of his motives.

Eventually I found a job as a secretary for the vice president of a bank in Dover. I made friends with several women I worked with and was close to two in particular. One woman, Ilene, was slightly older than my mother. Her kids were the same age as Tom and me. The other woman, Heidi, and I were a few years apart in age. Tom and I would get together with Heidi and her husband Clark all the time. We went to concerts, bars and the local fair in the fall. We would also take turns hosting dinner parties.

Just shy of our first anniversary, I received a call from my mother. My cousin Michael had committed suicide. He blew his brains out. I was in absolute shock. I couldn't fathom Michael, who thought he was God's gift to women, shooting himself in the head.

For our first anniversary, Tom and I went to the Bostonian Hotel for cocktails to start, then a carriage ride around the city from Faneuil Hall and dinner at the famous French restaurant, Maison Robert, featured in the Folgers commercials in the '80s. I will never forget that night. While waiting for our table, we had champagne at the bar. Once we were seated, I looked around the restaurant and began to observe the people. One table next to us had a family with two young children. Tom and I saw how stuffy the family seemed and how proper the kids were. This restaurant was known for all the famous people who ate there like John Wayne and Elton John.

We started out with some beluga caviar and while we were eating, the funniest thing happened. A mouse ran out from under another table, across the floor, and Tom and I saw it. Tom, who obviously had too much to drink at that point, stood up and yelled "Who let the mouse in without a tux?" The kids next to us started to giggle and their parents quickly reprimanded them. It was like *The Blues Brothers*! I was laughing so hard, I almost peed my pants! The waiter ran over to our table and Tom repeated what he said, and the bus boys were trying to catch the mouse. It was hilarious! They ended up not charging us for the caviar. It was times like this that I could almost overlook Tom's indiscretions, almost being the key word.

But the stress of our marriage was weighing heavily. Deep down I knew I didn't want this kind of a marriage. This was how Joe acted for the first 8 years or so of my parents' marriage. That was my reality. I was reliving my parents' marriage and I felt angry and betrayed. When Tom and I argued, and I felt the need to get away, Tom would take my keys from me and not give them back. This would go on until I eventually gave up because I was too tired, tired of it all and mostly of Tom. It was all about control, which he had. All our money went into one account that I didn't have access to except when it was necessary. I had to produce receipts for everything and would be grilled on what I spent on a weekly basis.

Despite my growing concerns about the state of our marriage, we began to look for a house. We had spent almost two years in the duplex and were ready to move on. We settled for a ranch house located not far from the ocean in York, Maine. It had a little more than a half-acre and we had a creek that ran through it, which was an overflow for one of the inlets. It was a cute little ranch built in the '50s with all natural woodwork, and a breezeway with a tongue and groove ceiling. The breezeway eventually became a dining room because the kitchen didn't have enough room in it for more than four people at the table. I loved that house—it had a lot of charm.

We moved in the middle of the winter, with the help of Heidi and Clark, and my father. Clark would often comment on that move because my father, who was a heavy smoker, stopped to light a cigarette as they were carrying our refrigerator inside even as he labored to breathe. Clark thought that was comical. Dad liked that I was living in New England because he was stationed there in the service and had a good friend from New Hampshire. Shortly after we moved in, I found out I was pregnant.

As we acclimated to our new home, we prepared one of the bedrooms for the baby. The house was in mint condition when we bought it so it was just a matter of decorating and adding furniture. Tom's partying didn't slow down much. In fact, when I was eight months pregnant, he didn't bother to come home at all one night. Tom had mentioned where his boss was staying and I called there to find out where Tom was. I called there at 6 am. How embarrassing for everyone involved. Tom's boss said he had gotten a room. An hour later, I heard from Tom. He stayed because he had too much to drink, but that had never stopped him in the past and I doubt one would drink too much while they were with their new boss.

During my pregnancy, I was a nervous wreck. I really didn't want children and Tom knew that before he married me. My own experiences left me fearful of the whole parenting thing and to add insult to injury, Tom wanted me to go back to work after the baby was born. I vacillated throughout the pregnancy about this. Given my childhood, I couldn't fathom someone else raising my kids. The fear of someone touching my baby was more than I could bear. At the same time, I was scared to death that I would be a terrible parent. Tom knew very little of my past so he couldn't understand my fears leading up to the birth. One day Tom came home from work and told me to breast feed so he could save money on formula. One of the other guys he worked with had his wife breast feed their kids to save money. I don't know. I guess it was the fact that he TOLD me I had to do it so he could save money. I said, Fuck You! I went with formula.

A week and a half after our third anniversary, our son, Justin, was born. Tom was very attentive, but left three days later on a business trip. My mother showed up shortly after Justin's birth. She was all about grandkids; probably because she could admire but not be responsible for them. God knows she never took responsibility for us when we were growing up. After she left and we were back to our schedule, I fell into a deep post-natal depression. I was all alone with no idea how to raise this beautiful little boy. I had nightmares regularly and the lack of sleep didn't help. Justin cried non-stop for the first nine months. He would only take twenty minute naps and never slept for more than that. I thought I was going to lose my mind.

When summer arrived, I packed up the car and Justin, and then headed to the beach. As a resident, we had season passes. I love the water even though I had almost drowned once as a kid. At the beach I had met another woman, Katie, with her son, Ryan, who was exactly one year older than Justin. We became close friends and met every day on the beach. Tom and I would get together with her and her husband John. The kids were like brothers. We celebrated Justin's first birthday with them and our friend, Ilene, who was like a grandmother to Justin. I was creating a nice family. Ilene replaced my mother as grandmother and Katie was the sister I never had. Tom's late nights out drinking slowed down. He still went out from time to time with the excuse that he had to take his customers out. It was part of his job, but he was home most nights. And I was at a safe distance from my family where no one could "drop in." So that was a good thing.

Tom's parents would come and visit for a few days at a time. I didn't really get along with them. Over the years I grew to dislike his father; he was a bastard. The guy was brutal. There wasn't anything you could say or do that that guy wouldn't criticize. He had to always be right. My mother-in-law couldn't even speak without being corrected. Ever! He insulted and belittled everyone. Tom's way of dealing with his father was to totally shut down. To make matters worse, I fought with my father-in-law because I could see that he was nothing more than a blowhard that talked too much. He would get your thoughts twisted so much so that you couldn't remember what you were arguing about. I would look to Tom for some support but he would be totally zoned out. He never stood up for me or himself, for that matter. After belittling or criticizing, his father would say, "I'm just talking." Tom would say the same thing, not realizing he sounded just like his father. Tom always hated it when his father would say that, too. My father-in-law also demanded that we be at his house every Christmas. It didn't matter that we had a small child and I wanted to be home in our house so that Justin could enjoy the day. His father would tell me that Christmas was for adults. I hated it and Tom knew, but he refused to even broach the subject. Needless to say, the relationship between his parents and me was strained.

On the other hand, my father would never travel on Christmas when we were kids. His parents always had to come to our house. In his opinion, Christmas was for the kids. Christmases in our house didn't always turn out so well when I was young. When we lived in the city, he passed out under the tree while setting up a train set for us. And there were the Christmas Eves that he would come home and beat my mother. But despite all that, he always had the presents wrapped and under the tree. My father would stay up all night Christmas Eve and wrap if he had to. Considering the fact that he had very little to do with children, he loved Christmas. It was his time to shine. I guess this was his way of making up for all the hell he caused.

On the other hand, my mother hated wrapping. If she had her way, the presents would have been thrown under the tree still in the shopping bags. She even said as much. In fact, she did that for my birthday one year. I was in middle school sick with an ear infection that had me on the sofa for days. My birthday came and my mother, who had just come home from her part time job at the pharmacy, handed me a brown shopping bag. I opened the bag and looked in to see a couple of ropes of rock candy. I glanced over at her and she said, "Happy Birthday" and walked away. To this day, I have a very hard time on my birthdays.

Because of Tom's unilateral decision-making and lack of respect for my opinion, resentment was growing in our relationship. Despite that and other pressing issues, I pursued what I thought was the happy family. We would drive to Bar Harbor at least once a year to go wind jamming, drive around the harbors and walk around Cadillac Mountain or we would spend time in the White Mountains in New Hampshire. I still can't make up my mind if I prefer living on the ocean or in the mountains. I enjoy both almost equally.

My friendship with Katie grew. The following summer it was time to register Justin for preschool. We decided to go with the school Katie and John had Ryan in. It was a hard decision because it was a bit of a drive, but it was supposed to be the best in the area. I was also pregnant with our second child.

Every day, I drove Justin back and forth. The school was great and I was meeting more of Katie's friends. March rolled around and our daughter, Kylie was born. I went into labor in the middle of the night. Our friend Ilene was our go-to person to watch Justin. I called her and waited for her to arrive then we headed to the hospital. The minute Kylie was born I looked at Tom and told him if he ever laid a finger on her, I would kill him. He was stunned. He said that was one hell of a way to talk to your husband, but I wasn't taking any chances. It's not as if I thought he would do anything because I didn't. I just wasn't taking ANY chances!

Tom decided he was going back to school for his MBA. He was accepted to Northeastern University so while he worked, he wined and dined customers, went to classes and spent weekends doing homework. I was left to raise the kids and take care of everything else. My friendships with Katie, Tracy (a friend I met through Katie) and Ilene were paramount to me; they were my support. I relied on them more than Tom. If I went to Tom for help with the kids he would say I was on my own. That was extremely apparent the time I had appendicitis. I had a warning the week before it actually happened but didn't pay attention. I had dropped Justin off at school and went shopping. I was at the drugstore looking at cards for Kylie's birthday. I began to feel a sharp pain in my lower abdomen. I started to rub it thinking it was a gas pain but the pain increased to the point where I doubled over in the aisle. I had Kylie in the cart so not knowing what was happening, I carefully and slowly pushed the cart to the restroom. I had all I could do to open the door. Standing there was an employee. She took one look at me and ran over to help me in and held the door so I could see Kylie. The woman wanted to call an ambulance but I refused. I told her I had to pick up my son and was running late because of the pain. I stood in the bathroom massaging my stomach until I could move. I painfully exited the store without making a purchase and was late picking up Justin. That night when Tom arrived home, I told him what had happened but we shrugged it off.

The following week on St. Patrick's Day, the pain started again. This time I called my OBGYN. They took me right in. After a sonogram my doctor came in and said that they found a large cyst on my ovary the size of a lemon but he didn't think that was my problem. He ordered blood work. He suspected my white blood cells were high. He thought I was having an appendicitis attack and said he wouldn't be surprised if I was in the emergency room by the end of the day.

I drove home with the kids and tried to not think about it. That evening when Tom was home, I told him what the doctor said. He asked how I was feeling. I was in pain but nothing worth going to the ER for. So we had dinner and carried on with the nightly routine. By 10 pm, I couldn't handle it anymore. I called Ilene and she came over to watch the kids while Tom drove me to the ER. At 2:00 in the morning, the doctors took my appendix out. Tom was in the recovery room with me. He said he was headed home to relieve Ilene, get Justin ready for school, shower and grab something to eat. He did that and returned later that morning with Kylie. He sat her on the bed with me and said he had to make some calls for work and would be right back. He returned three hours later. He left Kylie with me. What two-year old is going to sit still in a hospital? The woman next to me couldn't believe it. I was hooked up to an IV recovering from surgery and my husband left our two-year old with me. I understood that we didn't have family to help but you would think he would have called his boss and explained the situation and stayed home. Not Tom. Work came first, always did, still does.

To be fair, Tom would fit the kids in when he could. The nights he was home at a reasonable hour, he would read them bedtime stories, which was huge in our house. He spent time with Justin building Lego castles and forts, and he would sit with Kylie in her room while she put rollers in his hair or played with her tea bunnies. One year he was a soccer coach for Justin's team and I was his assistant. So in between the craziness of his schedule, he would find some time to play with them.

I muddled through those years while Tom was engrossed in work and his MBA; I spent a lot of time with Katie and Tracy. We would take turns having parties at each other's homes and the kids loved spending time with Jim, Tracy's husband. He was great with them. Justin in particular was close to Jim. Tom had a couple of close friends through work that we would get together with as well. As our network of friends grew, I became comfortable. For the first time in my life, I felt like I had a "real" family. That's what I was looking for, a family that wasn't mine. With Kylie in preschool and Justin in a private school in New Hampshire, I had some free time to myself. I felt great, I had a circle of friends, the kids were doing well, and we had a nice life on the coast.

After Tom graduated from Northeastern with an MBA, I went back to school. Since I had a knack for design and it was one of the few degrees the school offered, I decided I would go for that. I was doing real well too, straight A's. The woman that taught most of the design classes thought I should be running my own company.

My world came crashing down when Tom announced he was looking for another job because his company had overlooked him for a manager's position. I agreed despite my concerns about moving and selling the house I loved that was in a perfect location. I had one request. I told him I did not want to move back to the Albany area. Although the company he was working for was based in Albany, his position was in New England. He started to apply for jobs and contact headhunters. He interviewed for a position in Kentucky but that didn't pan out. Then another opportunity presented itself. Guess where? Albany! He interviewed but didn't think it went well. He doesn't handle stress well so when he didn't hear back from them right away, he said they didn't like him. He walked around the house slamming things and swore to himself. He wasn't enamored with having to continue the search. They did get back to him and offered him the position. I didn't want him to take it, but it was a big promotion and he really wanted it.

After he accepted the position, reality set in that the house would have to go on the market. I couldn't bring myself to do it. I loved everything about the area, and the ocean. I refused. I begged him to figure out how to keep the house and maybe move into something smaller so we could afford both. Having a house on the New England coast isn't something you just give up.

So Tom embarked on a campaign to make me feel bad. He accused me of being a rotten mother if I didn't let him take the job and move because I would be denying our family the higher income. He said I was a terrible wife for not wanting him to do better. This constant barrage of insults went on for days. I finally gave in. I cried as I signed the seller's agreement. Our house sold within six hours of putting it on the market. Did we set the price too low? Maybe a little, but the market wasn't doing well at the time. Now, I half joke that we can't afford to buy our own house back.

With the house sold the first day on the market, the rush to find something in Albany was put on me and I didn't want to be there in the first place. The housing market there wasn't doing well either; the inventory was terrible. I didn't want to be near my family, so I tried to look in the surrounding areas outside the city. I looked at one place that had a great two acre lot but the house was an utter mess. There were holes in the walls, trashy carpets, dented baseboard heat, and it needed a new roof. It was horrible so I said no. The house across the street, however, was awesome but a little small so I hemmed and hawed about it. I asked my father to take a look at it, which he did. Unfortunately he found an issue with the electricity which was a fire hazard. But before we could negotiate something with the owner, another couple put in an offer that was accepted.

So with that, I was back to square one. I was flying back and forth looking at properties as Tom was winding down his current position. The new company was paying for the move so it wasn't an issue of packing but just finding a house. Inventory wasn't improving and I had to go back and look at properties I had already said no to. That included the one that had been on the market for two years because of its condition.

Tom decided to take a look. He agreed it was trashed but the property was nice. He promised I could hire a contractor to do work on it before moving in. So we lowballed the owners who were truly desperate to be rid of it. They accepted. I was going all out though. I decided that if I had to give up my home on the coast, I was putting in what I wanted and there would be no argument. I went to the local junkyards on the coast to locate cast iron radiators to replace the trashed baseboard. I hired a contractor to rip out all the carpeting and install hardwood floors and tile. I hired another contractor to install a top of the line German boiler and the cast iron radiators I had purchased in Portsmouth. Then I hired a window contractor to install new windows. The roof was taken care of by the owners as part of the sale.

The day arrived for the closing on our house in Maine. We took the kids to spend the night with Tracy and Jim. They loved Jim, he would take them to the local children's museum where he worked and let them run around. Tom and I stayed in a hotel then drove that morning to take one last look around to make sure we had everything. Then we stopped at Tracy and Jim's to see the kids before heading to the bank. When we walked into the bank, I began to feel sick, like something was wrong kind of sick. It was gut-wrenching. I sat at the table with the couple buying our house, the lawyers and the bank representative. They were laughing and happy they were getting such a nice house. In fact, the woman even said to me that my decorating and maintenance of the home were the reasons she wanted it!

Tom was happy because he was moving into a new position that came with a higher salary. They were all happy except for me. My eyes welled with tears as I looked around and listened to the woman compliment me on the house. As the papers started to circulate around the table and everyone was signing, I could feel my lips start to tremble. I burst out crying and ran out of the room, down the stairs and out the door to the car. Tom ran out behind me. I was shaking but he insisted I sign and said we had to move and that was that. He thought that once I did the work to the new house, all would be good. For him, it was about his career and money. It took me 20 minutes to calm myself down enough to walk back in. The woman said she understood why I was upset; giving up a beautiful home was hard. She had no idea that it was more than the house for me. It was what I had built, a new family and life far away from my old family. A place where I felt safe, at least, as safe as someone like myself could feel. Something I had never experienced in my life up until then and it was being ripped away. My marriage died for me that day and with it, a part of me.

Chapter 4

PART 2

Because of all the construction going on in the house, we had to stay at a Residence Inn. I traveled back and forth and spent most days cleaning and working with the contractors. The kids played outside or stayed with my in-laws. Dad would stop by to monitor the guy installing the new boiler and cast iron radiators. Not sure he appreciated the 'supervision' but he wasn't going to say no to my father. In addition to the work around the house, we transferred Justin to his new school and after some research, found a preschool for Kylie, just in the nick of time for the school year.

While staying at the Residence Inn, we met a family that Tom's company, headquartered in France, had relocated from Rouen. They were there on a three-year contract. Because of the housing market, they were having a difficult time finding a place to live so they were held up like us. They had two kids the same age as ours, the oldest, a boy and the youngest, a girl, so it was a perfect match for Justin and Kylie. They didn't know any English, so it was a challenge at first. After a day at the house working, the kids and I would return to the inn around four. I would get them changed and go down to the pool to cool off. Corrine would do the same with their kids. Justin and Kylie would play with them in the pool and shoot hoops. Through their play and watching Disney movies, it was amazing how fast the kids learned to speak English.

A month went by and we were finally able to move into the house. Our belongings had been stored in the moving truck all that time. I was worried about what kind of shape our furniture and other items would be in after sitting in a hot semi for a month. In addition to our belongings, we had made an arrangement with our friends in Hyannis Port to buy their furniture and have the moving company pick it up and drive it to our house. So we had to coordinate the actual move with two different trucks and a large crew. Aside from the ongoing renovations, the house was beginning to look like a New England home.

Our first weekend, Labor Day weekend, in the house was a disaster. The area was hit with a storm that felt more like a tornado. The night before Labor Day we had gone to bed—at the time it was only a thunderstorm with heavy winds, but after midnight, all that changed. We were asleep when the top of one of the maple trees on the side of the house sheared off and hit the house squarely between Justin and Kylie's bedroom windows. The force of the tree hitting the house woke Kylie out of a sound sleep. We woke to her screaming. After settling her down, we looked to see what made all the noise, but couldn't see what had hit the house since we had already lost power.

The next morning we woke to devastation. The storm had even killed someone in a campground. For the first time ever a local fair had to close. Area businesses lost roofs, and a large swath of homes lost power, including us. Luckily, the only damage we had was the tree that hit the house.

When my father heard the news, he drove over with a generator. We were able to plug in the fridge. I had to use our grill to cook, using the side burner for coffee and a cast iron griddle to make pancakes and grilled cheese. It was a week before our power was restored. Kylie was afraid to go to bed after that. We had to leave her closet light on from then on.

Once all the power was back on, the kids were finally able to start school. For the first six months or so I worked on the house, painting, cleaning, and repairing. Much to my surprise, no one showed up unannounced including my in-laws. Even though my mother lived close by, she rarely showed up. She was busy studying for a theology degree to become a minister. Imagine my surprise. My father and in-laws lived north of the city so it was a longer drive for them. I made friends with neighbors. Their kids were the same age as Justin and Kylie. In the fall, I continued my education at the local community college. Following my passion for design, I signed up for their architectural drafting degree which included a few classes in basic interior design as well.

Once I started school, my time became consumed with drafting and model building. There was no time for play. I had to rely on Tom to do things with the kids, a switch in our relationship that he wasn't prepared for, but he did the best he could. It was the most time he had ever spent with them. But he wasn't much help with work around the house. He did yard work, which he didn't mind so he kept up with that, but the rest was up to me. I tried to manage classes, kids and housework. I scheduled my classes around Kylie's pre-school, which was not an easy task. Between the move, renovations and major workload for my design classes, I was running on empty by the following Christmas. My mother had bought the kids tickets to see Wizard of Oz on ice. We were supposed to go as a group, but I was in overdrive and had worked through what I thought was a cold. The day of the event, I woke up and couldn't move. I stood up and went to pick up the laundry basket to take down to the laundry and I couldn't lift it. I fell to the floor and just sat there. Tom got out of bed and helped me downstairs. I crawled up on the sofa while he made coffee. I couldn't breathe, my back hurt every time I took a breath or coughed.

Mom watched the kids while Tom drove me to the emergency room. I had bronchial pneumonia. Tom took the kids to the show with my mother while I slept on the sofa for the rest of the day. That was a rough Christmas. To hear the kids talk about it now is funny because whenever Tom had to take care of them as in actually cook a meal, he would give them Kraft Mac & Cheese, peanut butter and jelly sandwiches, a can of soup or grilled cheese. Kylie would have to tell him how to make it.

By spring I had noticed a difference in Tom. He was not interested in our relationship intimately; this from someone who did not take no for an answer. At first I thought it was because I was so busy with school and the kids. I was always running around cleaning or transporting someone, and if I wasn't doing that, I was in my drafting room. I discovered why that fall when we attended a coworker's party. As we entered the house and were greeted by our host, a woman ran up to him, kissing him. As I made my way around the party and into the kitchen our friend from Paris and his wife were there. He took one look at me and started to back into the wall. He was worried about what I would do; everyone in the house saw what the woman had done. I found myself in yet another embarrassing situation thanks to Tom. You would think another huge red flag would have gone off—it did, but I was so engrossed in my drafting classes that I blew it off.

Tom, the coyote, was signaling yet again that he couldn't be trusted. He was an opportunist and pathological liar, and I wasn't recognizing it. Why? Was it because I was so used to my mother's lies and deceit? Or that I was so used to being a victim that it became increasingly difficult to recognize bad behavior. Not long after the party, I heard the woman had left the company. I don't know the details about her departure. I do know that one of the company executives was there the night of the party. I was good friends with his wife and they witnessed what happened; maybe something was said. Tom wouldn't talk about it.

By then, we had formed a pretty tight-knit group with Tom's co-workers who had started their jobs around the same time. Most of them had moved from other states. Our friends from Paris would come to our house for cookouts and holidays. The kids became good friends. Much to my surprise, our own families didn't show up unannounced so I was able to manage their visits well enough. During the breaks I did get, I would travel as often as possible to Maine to visit Tracy, Jim and the kids. Despite the distance, we remained very close. Everyone knew that I wanted to move back there.

Surprisingly, my relationship with my father had improved. I always felt sorry for him. I knew he was lonely and I couldn't stand that thought even though I knew what he was capable of and I knew it was his own doing, but a part of me wanted a father, the one I never had growing up and on some level, once I married Tom, he seemed to step into that role. He liked Tom and we did as much as we could to accommodate Dad. He visited us on a regular basis and attended holiday dinners. He didn't have any friends; he didn't have anything to do with Jeff and Bill, and all of his brothers lived out of state. I was his only family. He sold his houseboat and had recently retired so most of his time was spent putzing around his house. When he was around, I was very careful about leaving the kids alone with him. It was a conscious decision since I still wasn't able to see the face of the man who abused me, so I wasn't taking chances. It was always a precarious situation for me but he seemed happy to spend time with us.

True to form, however, we had a major blowout the summer of 1999. It started out innocently enough. He asked me to meet him at a house he was interested in buying. When I arrived, I stepped out of the car leaving Justin and Kylie in the backseat momentarily while I walked towards him. I noticed the backyard had a steep slope towards the backyards of two adjacent houses with kids running around yelling and screaming. Now, my father didn't like kids and he certainly didn't like people being too close, so you could imagine my surprise when I saw the layout.

In addition, he had severe health issues and couldn't even shovel the two steps he had where he was living at the time. This property was further out into the countryside with no store or hospital close by. And, it was further into the snow-belt. All of this was running through my head as I surveyed the situation and because I was quick to spell out the "cons" to living there, he exploded! He started yelling, saying I was always too hard to please. That made me cringe, and it still makes me cringe to this day. Then he said he was just going to drive home and blow his brains out.

He jumped into his jeep and stepped on the gas just like Jeff's graduation party and barreled past me, almost hitting my car with the kids in it. He drove across the front lawn of this house, hit the ditch and the jeep went airborne! I stood in shock, but quickly scanned the area for the kids who were out playing. I ran to my car to check on Justin and Kylie who were watching the event unfold. They were upset but okay. I drove home and called my mother who suggested I call social services. They sent the police to his house to check on him.

He called me yelling that I had sent the police after him. I told him that I called social services and they were the ones who called the police. I explained that I was worried he would really shoot himself but he told me to go fuck myself. That was the last time I ever saw my father alive. He ended up buying a house in the nearby city of Schenectady. A year later Jeff, my brother, received a call from him. Dad told him he was moving and that if he wanted anything, he should get his ass over that morning to get it. Jeff went and Dad told him to tell everyone to fuck off. Dad wouldn't say where he was going, but he had his jeep packed and a trailer attached. Everything else was at the end of his driveway in the garbage, including all the model ships he had painstakingly built and loved.

Speaking of Jeff, he visited us a few times. It was difficult to get him to go outside his self-imposed world. I thought that we might have a shot at getting him out of his shell because he loved seeing Justin and Kylie, but he was too far gone. His state of mind wouldn't allow him to visit or stay for very long. He was always paranoid and worried about someone seeing him, like one of our neighbors stopping by. He was also ashamed of what Justin and Kylie thought of him. He had zero communication skills and would explode like Dad. I suppose showing up the few times he did took a tremendous toll on him. When he did visit, he would sit for an hour or so with the kids and play; naturally they thought the world of Uncle Jeff. Jeff has been sober since the kids were little and I'm proud of him for doing that, but he continues to smoke pot and cigarettes. Knowing we didn't do either, he felt guilty about that too. He didn't want the kids to smell it. We couldn't even get him to come over for the holidays. He came close once but he didn't want to see Dad.

Shortly after Kylie's birth, Bill had left the state for the south. He became a crack addict and was caught holding up a convenience store to finance his habit. In order to avoid jail, he gave state's evidence and the 'drug ring' he dealt with was arrested as a result. When they found out it was him, they threatened to kill him so he skipped state. We saw him once at Christmas (1999) when he risked coming back so my mother could see his son who was nine months old at the time.

After four short years, everything came crashing down. A manager's position had opened in the marketing department and Tom was certain he qualified for it. The position was given to a younger guy. Tom was devastated but mostly envious. He started to talk to our neighbor, who owned his own company, about a marketing position with him as well as part ownership. They talked for several months before they were comfortable with the transition. Tom had made the decision to resign.

It was fall by the time all of this happened. I was worried, even suggesting that Tom rethink his decision because our neighbor was not a nice guy. Our dog didn't even like him. Every time he would come over, our dog would bark and growl. To me that was a clear sign that the guy was not a good person, but Tom resigned anyway. He was too green with envy, pissed that he wasn't even given a chance to interview for the job and no one was going to stop him, especially me. To him, I was nothing more than a maid and my words had no weight. It was a repeat of when he belittled me into selling our house in Maine. I was the bad guy for not supporting him because God knows I hadn't supported him up till then.

Nine months later, the partnership dissolved and Tom was out of work. He was a basket case and no one could talk any sense into him. He was hysterical beyond hysterical. His father pulled me aside one day and expressed concern. I understood completely. I lived with him and that was how he reacted when something didn't go right and it didn't matter what that something was, he could have been repairing a lawn mower or light fixture and his reaction would have been the same—totally unreasonable. He would babble to himself and would not listen. He shut down just like he would every time his father would talk or should I say, criticize. That's when I realized that there was something else at play, that possibly the wires weren't connecting for him. I had those thoughts in the past but this situation exaggerated it to the point that there was no denying his state of mind. Tom just wasn't responding to anyone. I thought he was having a mental breakdown.

He started looking for work immediately and was offered two positions at the same time within a few weeks. One of them would have kept us in the Albany area but it was in a different field much like what he had just experienced with our neighbor; the other was in Rochester and directly related to his field. I had some sway in this decision because I was of the opinion that although we would have to move yet again he should take the job in Rochester so that he could get back into his line of work. My reasoning managed to sink in and he took the job. He was not happy about it, as it meant a drastic cut in salary, selling our house and buying a new one—all for a sales position which was something he hadn't done in five years. It was totally beneath him but instead of being humbled by the whole situation, he went in the opposite direction and blamed everyone, including his new boss. He felt like everyone was conspiring to keep him down. This was reminiscent of my father, who was always paranoid. I started to worry that Tom would turn into a paranoia case and not recover from this transition.

We put our house on the market that summer and it sold before we found anything in Rochester. I attributed it to my awesome design ideas and the fact that it really was a great piece of land. We had to make the deal contingent upon finding something ourselves. Tom, in this case, pretty much let me decide what and where to buy because I made a killing on the sale of our home. I chose a home that I initially looked at when I first started the search. It was a very unique custom build with a bit of a Frank Lloyd twist, but it cost too much and needed massive updating. The house sat all summer and the owners were looking to get out, so we revisited and put in a low-ball offer. They countered and we met in the middle. It was still more than what we wanted to pay, but my eyes saw well beyond the massive updating. I would call it a diamond in the rough for sure.

Because it took so long to find a house, the closing fell on the Tuesday after Thanksgiving (2003), which meant that we had nowhere to stay for the holiday. A friend of my mother's offered to let us stay with her, so we moved most of our belongings into her basement and garage, the rest in a moving truck. We stayed that week with her. I cooked Thanksgiving dinner as a thank you for letting us stay. It isn't easy to put up a family of four and all their belongings. It was cramped but not terrible. It was very sweet of her, a retired 80 year-old nurse. She had been living alone for so long that she was just happy to have a house full of people again. It was a Thanksgiving to remember.

The following Monday we drove to Rochester and stayed in a hotel. We closed on the new house and moved in on December 3rd! Being the good mom that I am, I had diligently packed all holiday items accordingly so that when we unpacked, I was able to decorate the house immediately in hopes of lessening the trauma of the move for the kids. It was already disastrous with respect to school, pulling them from one school district and moving them into another during the holidays! Miraculously, I was able to pull it off, but it was a massive drain. After the holidays I pretty much vegged for a few weeks. I was in no hurry to do much of anything; the weather was miserable anyway. I was totally disoriented in the house. It had big windows that look out over the countryside and I would sit on the sofa with a cup of coffee in the morning and watch the school buses. Due to a bridge closure, which eliminated one of the routes to our home, it took me a few weeks to figure out the roads.

By mid-January I was bored, so while the kids were at school, I started to explore our new surroundings. I stumbled upon a secondhand store that had recently opened and struck up a conversation with the woman manager. I told her that we had recently moved to the area and that I was an antique junkie. The store had just opened but they were expecting to be full up by the end of the month. I frequented the store throughout the winter and early spring. By summer I was working there as an assistant manager.

Justin and Kylie were slowly getting adjusted to their new school and Tom was schlepping, as he liked to call it, around doing his thing. When I wasn't working at the store, I was working on renovations both inside and outside the house, not to mention trying to keep up with the basic everyday cleaning. The house was huge, so much so that when it was built, it had an intercom system which had long since stopped working. We would yell from the rotunda, which was in the center of the house, because everything seemed to reverberate from there. It was the only way we could hear each other.

By 2005, Tom asked me to start looking for a full time job. He hated what he was doing; the cut in pay and crappy benefits didn't help and he was still reeling from his experience with the partnership so his paranoia was worse than ever. He would feel better if I had some kind of benefits to fall back on "just in case something went wrong." He made our lives a living hell though. When he was home, he constantly complained about his job and how he had to schlep around and how he worried about money. He kept up with the yard work and garbage detail, but that was about it. He wasn't any fun to be around at all. The kids would ask me if their father knew how to laugh. In fact, I can probably count how many times I've actually heard him laugh. I certainly couldn't have a normal conversation with him. I was isolated more so than ever before. Then I finally got a job with a PR firm in the city of Rochester the following August.

In the spring of 2006, I decided to go back to school and finish my degree. It was a struggle to work full time, take a class, and keep up with the house and kids. Being isolated didn't help either. I had built such a wall around myself, that I wasn't paying attention to me anymore. I was trying to survive the circumstances and I didn't want to get involved with neighbors or co-workers. I didn't trust people so the idea of making friends once again was just too much. So, I put my head down and went to work, ignoring my surroundings.

The relationship with my mother reached a new low too. Through her ministry she started counseling prisoners at a maximum security prison. She developed a close relationship with one prisoner, divulging all the details of our family members. Imagine my shock when I learned he knew my address and all about my children. That was when I decided I had enough of my mother.

At the same time Tom and I were struggling. Tom remained distant as he grew more and more discontent with his job. The kids were involved in activities and we did take a few vacations here and there, the typical Universal Studio and Disney stuff. My schedule was grueling, but I had to stay on track; my goal was to complete my degree before Justin finished college.

Mid-December 2006, I received word from a colleague of Tom's in Albany that his old job had become available and that they wanted him back. So I mentioned my conversation with our friend to Tom. I told him that his job was open, but he was reluctant to call them. He said he didn't want to go through the process only to be rejected. "What? She is telling you that they want you to come in." We went back and forth about this until after the first of the year.

Finally, I convinced him to call his colleagues. He drove to Albany and talked with them. When he came back from the interview he sounded enthusiastic but not confident because in Tom's eyes it is always doomsday. A few weeks later he was offered his old job back. There was just ONE minor detail—we lived in Rochester. Tom's solution was to drive to Albany on Monday mornings and stay at his parents during the week, then drive back Friday nights. I told him that it was a bad idea to split up the family and that long distance doesn't work for relationships especially when you have kids. Justin was just entering high school and Kylie was turning 13 which is a very sensitive age for a young girl.

I would have moved, but Tom refused to let me quit my job, which I hated. It was secretarial in nature. He was all about the money and the benefits. The thing is, the kids were old enough to see that and they did. I agreed to the commute with the understanding that it would be temporary until we could figure out what to do.

Before Kylie's 13th birthday in 2007, Tom was working and living in Albany and driving back on the weekends. We argued constantly about selling the house and moving. He refused because of the cost. I knew that it wasn't just that; he was making more than he did when he left there. By that summer, his father told him that he was no longer allowed to stay with them during the week because he thought what Tom was doing to our family was wrong. So, if you can stand it, Tom asked my mother if he could stay with her. I was furious! I told him that if he insisted on keeping the family apart it was going to lead to bad things and that he should rent an apartment if he refused to move us there. I said if you want this job so damn bad, then pay for an apartment, but he wouldn't part with the money or sell the house. I considered his decision a separation, which it was. He was only visiting us on the weekends and when Justin would ask him to shoot hoops or play, Tom said he had to catch up on his paperwork first. Justin would wait all day for his father to spend time with him. Four o'clock would roll around and Tom would ask Justin if he was ready and Justin would just look at him like—are you kidding? Tom had disconnected from the family, and the resentment grew between him and the kids and with me. He wouldn't even call them during the week to talk to them. On the weekends, Tom was in his own little world. He would read the paper, do his paperwork and run his errands. The rest of us were just in the way. By that August, our relationship was dead for me. I was numb and I was isolated. All I did was take care of the kids, a huge house, go to work and attend classes. This was the final nail in the coffin, so to speak. I knew this was the beginning of the end. I had endured so much with him. The fact that he walked out and left me to take care of things and didn't seem to care was galling. It felt like he had moved on to a new chapter in his life which I had a helping hand in and I was stuck in the old one.

Chapter 5

MY SURVIVAL

The pack was established and settled in a new territory. "The coyotes' territory is defined as the "home range," which is typically defended by the pack but not necessarily the mating pair." (Grady 39,) This is not part of the life cycle but simply a way of life. I can best explain my quest this way: Survival! A coyote's life is about survival, and they are pretty darn good at it. "Coyotes are highly adaptable and prove their tenaciousness by their sheer proliferation in our cities." (Cadieux, 210) Despite the odds, coyotes survive. This chapter and pretty much the rest of this book is about **my** survival. My quest began in the fall of 2007.

One day my massage therapist, a very spiritual human being who also practices reiki and chakra healing, asked me to think back to when I was a child and think about a happy moment. I had been going to her pretty much since we moved to the Rochester area. I asked, how far back? She said, as far back as you can remember. I thought about it for a while, then I asked, what if I can't think of a happy moment from my childhood? She said, "then that is your problem." It was her way of telling me that my back problems were a result of unresolved issues and that she couldn't help me until I helped myself.

A coworker was bragging about a new book and recommended it to everyone listening. So I thought I would give it a try. Let me pause for a moment here, as I will not apologize for what I am about to say. The book essentially said that everything that happens to you is your fault. I immediately threw the book away. I will say this only once; if ANYONE tells you that it's your fault that you were sexually abused as a child—THROW THEM AND THE BOOK OUT!!! When someone tells me that I was abused because of something I did from a previous life, I have just one thing to say: BULLSHIT! I will not accept that I was sexually abused because of something I may have done 500 years ago… It's a load of CRAP!!! There, now I have that off my chest…

Needless to say, I didn't read the book but knew I had to deal with "it" sooner or later but as usual, I put "it" back into its compartment. You see, throughout my marriage up to this point, I had put all the abuse in its own compartment. I didn't deal with it on any level. But now, I was beginning to make real strides to facilitate change, like finishing my degree for one. Up to that point, I knew things weren't right, but like most people, I stayed in my comfort zone. Change, who wants change? That would require us to step outside our boxes. And boy, did I build a box. I boxed myself in so much so that I didn't have anyone to turn to. I couldn't trust anyone. I didn't know how. So there I was, barely keeping my head above water; I started to ask myself "how did I get here?" All I know is I had this overwhelming feeling deep down inside that something or someone was fighting to get attention. Low and behold it was me, the real me. The one that had been stuffed down so far that the battle to get out wasn't going to be pretty. I was fighting back with every ounce of energy and stubbornness, and all my "toughness" that helped me survive. But things were different this time. Deep down, I knew I had to change, that I had to let her out, but the question was how? To make matters worse in the midst of this battle, a Trickster entered my life! Yes, another coyote but this one was different, or was he? I needed to find out.

Against my better judgment, Tom and I agreed to the new work arrangement. I remember like it was yesterday what I did after that decision. I was home alone; I had been thinking about it all day and as I walked around the house, I found myself standing before the Virgin Mary statue that sat on a bookshelf. It's my little prayer corner. I used her to collect lucky coins and prayer cards. I stood there looking at her and in my hand I happened to have a penny I had found heads up. I must have been walking around with it. I took the coin and tossed it in the planter part of the statue with the rest of the coins and said to myself that I would give it a shot and see what happens, but someone is going to come along and love me for who I am and want to spend time with me, do things with me, and more importantly respect me, my intelligence and communicate with me like the adult that I am. Then I mumbled to myself that it would be someone at work. I wasn't thinking of anyone in particular, not even a name; it just came out.

We had been 'separated' since before Kylie's birthday and it was now fall. There was zero indication from Tom that the situation was going to change. He was adamant that we were not going to sell the house and move. He continued to stay with my mother and drive back and forth. I was working, taking classes and taking care of the kids, the house and the pets.

While we were going through these major family changes, as part of my job, I helped out with PR functions throughout the year. Despite my previous apprehensions about making friends, I did make friends with a few of the people in my department as well as others. I also allowed myself to become friends with a few of our neighbors. Chris, a professional musician, would come over to the house one night a week and we would sit, drink wine and talk about what was going on in our lives. On occasion, Tom and I would get together with Chris and her husband, Alex.

As my responsibilities changed at work, I became more involved in working client functions for the department and was reintroduced to a colleague, Nathan. I didn't really get to know him until I was asked to work these functions. He was handsome with a captivating smile. Whenever he laughed, I would get chills up my spine. He was easy to talk to and seemed genuinely interested in what I had to say. I was totally attracted to him, but didn't realize it. In fact, he wasn't even on my radar.

I would run into Nathan as we passed each other in the hallways; we'd stop to chit chat and be on our way. A few months later, I ran into Nathan again at a conference where we spent more than the usual five minutes exchanging pleasantries. It was nice to talk to someone who genuinely communicated back, not only with conversation but with eye contact as well. We also shared some common ground by then. It just so happened that an intern who worked in my office also worked in his. So he would stop by periodically to see how the intern was doing. Not sure if the intern was an excuse or not, but I didn't mind. Nathan was a welcomed distraction. I felt an electrical current run up and down me every time we talked. The feeling was real and it was scary.

One rainy day our building had a fire drill. As we stood outside, I happened to spot Nathan with his crew. He ran over and offered up his umbrella. We stood together, waiting for the okay to re-enter the building. He told me about his about his ex, I wasn't sure whether he was referring to an ex-girlfriend or if he was divorced. Regardless, I put my arm around him, smiled and thanked him for being my savior.

A few weeks passed and I found myself at another conference, Nathan was looking for a seat and found one next to me. I was very naughty as I flirted terribly with him. I had a little too much wine but because I'm a bit older than him, I didn't take it seriously. Why would a younger guy be interested in me? I was over 40 so I thought he was just humoring me. As we gathered for the second half of the meeting, he walked past and gently brushed my arm. I almost died on the spot. My heart started to race, I could feel the blood rushing through my veins, and I felt flushed. As the night wore on, I wondered if I had imagined it. Was he flirting back? I started the usual routine of putting myself down. I thought he can't be interested in this tired old bitch, who by the way, happened to look very sexy that night. Then something worse occurred to me. As much as I wanted to dive in, and boy did I want to, I would be acting like my mother. The thought of that scared me more than anything else in the world. That is when my worlds collided. I wanted to be with Nathan so badly but my past came rushing back. Yes, I was unhappy, and my marriage was falling apart, but at the end of the evening, I drove home, confused and scared (but excited).

A couple of weeks later there was a talk given for a client. The topic was about being held hostage and the physical and sexual abuse of the women by a group of men (coyotes!). I thought maybe I would learn something. It never once occurred to me that Nathan would actually be there.

After the talk, Nathan stopped me to say hello and commented on how I was not there in my usual capacity. Meaning, I usually worked these types of events. I was obviously out of character dressed in jeans. The presentation had triggered something in me and I had to get out of there. As happy as I was to see him, I was more interested in getting some air. He followed me to the parking lot. We stopped to talk. I felt as though he wanted to say more but was holding back. In a way, so was I. There was no way I could tell him why I was really there. As we talked, we looked into each other's eyes and there was this connection between us. I could feel him reading me, the REAL me. That scared the hell out of me because I'm the one who reads people. I felt a pull towards him, but I said I should go and we parted ways.

As I drove home, I replayed it over and over. "Am I imaging this or is he flirting?" "Maybe he is only trying to be a good friend?" And the talk was more than I could handle. The little girl inside me was screaming to be let out but I was pushing her down, like, no stay inside! Worse, I felt a connection with Nathan, one I had never felt before in my life and as he leaned in towards me, I had wanted to kiss him. I don't know if he felt the same. Even being near Nathan was electrifying and scary to me.

When I arrived home, I poured a Jack Daniels and downed it. Then I poured another. Unfortunately after my third pour, I sent Nathan an email. I told him why I was there; that some of the abuse had actually happened to me. I felt safe in saying it. I can't explain it but there was something about him. That is saying a lot for me. I should have been able to say that about Tom! But I still didn't trust him with good reason.

So, now it was out. Nathan emailed me back almost right away and offered an ear anytime I felt like talking. The wall I had built around myself continued to collapse after that night.

A few months later, a client phoned looking to fill seats at a dinner party for his venue, so a coworker and I agreed to go. It was short notice and I had to come up with something to wear. I had purchased a red dress a few weeks earlier for a dinner with Tom. If I had thought seriously about the dress, I would have worn something else. I wasn't thinking about the implications. I admit it -- I am slow on the uptake at times and this was one of them. The day of the event, I brought the dress and change of shoes for that evening. Towards the end of the day, my coworker bailed on the dinner, as she couldn't find a sitter. That just left me and my red dress.

I arrived to the dinner a little late and when I walked into the room it became apparent that I was the only one there not in a black suit, white shirt and tie, and that included the few women that were there. There was one and only one exception and that was the speaker. He too was dressed in red. My heart stopped momentarily. I took a deep breath and stepped gingerly into the room with all eyes on me. My face was probably as red as the dress. I quickly went to the bar to get a Jack.

After I downed one I relaxed a little, and by the third

I didn't care. I sat at a table with some of the VPs. While dinner was being served, Nathan arrived. There was an empty chair at our table and he sat down. It was uncomfortable to say the least. He knew my secret and I was standing out like a sore thumb. As I tried to make conversation with the person next to me, my attention was diverted to the speaker who was obnoxiously pacing the room, chatting on his phone and generally being rude. Not only was I uncomfortable but my displeasure with the speaker was growing. At the end of the dinner I tended to a few work related things and returned to the bar. Nathan also walked up to get one more. He made some wiseass remark, and we laughed. When the speaker resumed his talk, I started to get the giggles. Nathan hushed me on several occasions, but I wasn't in the mood to listen. I had lost all respect during dinner. On top of that, my dress strap kept falling off my shoulder and I was constantly hoisting it back up. After the dinner, I decided it was time to head home. As I drove home, I replayed everything in my head, always over-analyzing.

    I had a routine on the mornings after I worked an event for a client. I would talk to the VP of Nathan's department. I didn't pull punches and usually told him what I thought. He liked that because I would make him laugh. So as usual, I went to his office to give him my opinion about the speaker. When I entered his office, he had a big grin on his face and was shaking his head. I asked what was up. He said I should not have worn a dress like that to the dinner. He had trouble concentrating with me sitting across from him dressed like that. I was too sexy and he wanted to jump me. As I began to grasp what he was saying, I started to back up towards the door. As I continued to back up, he jumped out of his chair, ran past me and shut the door! He picked me up in a bear hug and started kissing me. Naturally, I froze. He was attacking me and I wasn't able to do anything. I knew there was someone in the outer office who had heard at least the first part of what he said. When he let go of me, I fled.

When I got back to my office, I was shaking. My coworkers asked if I was okay, but how could I tell them that the VP down the hall had just molested me? I told Tom what happened when I spoke to him on the phone that night. Yes, it had been almost a full year and he was still commuting back and forth. Our marriage was severely strained but I thought he should know. Naturally he wanted me to turn the guy in to HR. But the question of how that would play out for me was in the back of my mind. This guy had been with the company a long time. Would I be the one punished? I was a mess for several days after. I stayed away from that part of the building as much as possible.

Two weeks later we were at another client event. I told Nathan what happened. He was upset and concerned but when I asked him what he thought I should do, he said he didn't think there was anything I could do. I was disappointed in his response because I thought he would have understood and been a little more supportive. While we stood by my car freezing, he looked into my eyes again and I looked back; he leaned in as if he was going to kiss me and stopped short. I complained I was freezing and should head home. I thought of the scene in Moonstruck where Ronnie (Nicholas Cage) led Loretta (Cher) to his apartment where they stood outside and she was complaining that she was freezing! Ronnie tells her to get in his bed. I knew that wasn't going to happen but deep down, I wanted him to scoop me up but he didn't and I was so cold, I couldn't stand it anymore. We parted ways yet again.

I never reported the VP and business went on as usual. Nathan and I ran into each other once in a while or I would stop in his office to say hello, but that was all. Spring sessions had ended and it was time to sign up for summer classes. My goal was to have my BA before Justin did. I thought the criminal justice class I chose would be fun but instead it was a huge trigger. It was as if the little girl in my past was haunting me. She was, and she wasn't letting go.

Criminal justice was a short class that required a research paper. I had never done a research paper before and the whole idea sent my stomach into knots. I had taken plenty of classes but they were in design, drafting and drawing. This class required a research paper and PowerPoint presentation. To make matters worse, the topic I chose was childhood sexual abuse. Why, you ask? Well, the book used for the class introduced a theory that I had a problem with. Much like the book I spoke about earlier, this theory had the same premise that the victim was to blame. As I leafed through the research books in the local library, I began to realize that most of them touched on parts of me, but none of them spoke to ME! As I sat there surrounded by books on the subject, I couldn't help but think that there I was—all laid out on that table—a little bit here, a little bit there, in essence puzzle pieces. I was a puzzle and the pieces had not been put together nor did they fit together. How depressing to sit there and realize that you are nothing more than an unassembled puzzle in desperate need of assembly. Basically, I had to ask, who am I?

I managed to put a paper and presentation together. I felt like an idiot because I was probably the only one in the class who had never done a research paper. On the final day of class, when the research paper and presentation were due, I ran into Nathan. He happened to be at the downtown library and was leaving with another woman, who I assumed was his newest love interest. I smiled and started to say hello but then realized he was walking right past without acknowledging me. Talk about a trigger! Do I need to emphasize how this affects us as survivors of sexual abuse? Treating us like we don't exist? To have Nathan treat me as all the other coyotes had, I didn't see that coming. But that was exactly what he did. I was mortified. Here I was about to present a paper on this kind of behavior and my so-called friend was treating me this way. I sat in a private area of the library. I couldn't believe what had just happened. Had I misjudged him? The answer here is probably a resounding yes because that's what survivors do. Unless we receive proper counseling, we seek out that which we know. In my heart I didn't want to believe it to be true. There was something about Nathan that seemed so genuine.

That sting lasted a while. I did not contact him nor did he stop by. Had the trickster shape-shifted? I was already living with one, was God sending me another? Would I ever learn to truly protect myself from the coyotes? Here I was, in my mid-forties and I still couldn't see them for what they are.

It was late August and every weekend there was some kind of festival going on. Justin and I had planned to go on Friday night to an Irish festival, but Tom insisted we wait until he could go with us the following night. He had not been home for the entire month. It seemed like there was always some reason why he was gone even on weekends. It was then that I suspected that he had yet another lover. When you don't come home on the weekends to see your own kids, something is up. Justin wasn't happy that his father wanted us to wait. To say the relationship between them was strained would be an understatement. Tom was never around and when he was, the kids weren't high priority for him. He was in another world when he was home. So Justin was not thrilled about spending time with his father, but I talked him into waiting.

The ride there was quiet, not much in the way of conversation. We walked around the festival to check out the vendors. We ran into a guy I knew from work. He had too much to drink and planted a big kiss smack on my lips along with a bear hug. Tom's jaw dropped, so I quickly introduced him as a friend. Once Tom realized he was drunk, he settled down. We bought a couple of beers and watched a band play. Tom wandered off, which was typical behavior. A little later he came back to inform me that one of our neighbors was there with his wife. I went over to say hello, and then returned to the table where we were standing. My intoxicated friend had joined us. The disgust on Tom's face was apparent.

As I sipped my beer and danced along to the music, I looked off to one side and standing at the next table was Nathan. My heart started to pound. I couldn't believe he was there. It took a couple of seconds to register that it was him. I smiled and he smiled back. Then he did something that threw me. He rushed over to talk to me. Surprised, I started to hyperventilate. He introduced the women he was with, one of whom was his girlfriend. Everything seemed to be moving in slow motion, but my body didn't seem to keep up. Then I felt a hand on my back tapping hard. I turned around and there was Tom with a look that could kill. I took a deep breath and introduced Nathan as a coworker. Tom went ballistic. At first, he started to sarcastically comment on the

T-shirt Nathan was wearing and then went on to say that he could see what was going on. He was yelling and turning beet red. Disgusted, Justin walked out of the building and I followed. Tom was two steps behind and continued his ranting. Justin walked back to the car. Totally embarrassed I walked away. I wanted to speak to Nathan, but there were no words to explain Tom's behavior. Instead I walked to the car. Justin and I waited for Tom; it was a silent ride home.

Once home, the argument escalated. I asked why he was so upset. He was the one after all that had not been home in a month. If anyone had any reason to suspect foul play, it would have been me. He said it was the way we looked at each other. It was in our eyes, he told me Nathan was waiting for me. He also called Nathan a pussy. The fact that Tom embarrassed me in front of a coworker was beyond belief. It was the typical double standard. Given his past history with women, Tom had zero room for accusations. The fact that my behavior was never once questioned didn't matter. Tom was the one who always drew attention from the opposite sex. Now the table was turned and he didn't like it. He forced himself on me, not for the first time, nor the last. It was his way of marking his territory.

After that night, Tom was even more distant. A few weeks went by; I had decided to enter a race with my newest running partner, a male coworker. The fact that I was running with this guy did not sit well with Tom, so he decided he was going to enter the race as well. I knew why he wanted to come along. I told him that my partner was happily married and that his wife was running with us, but that wasn't good enough.

The race took place early in the evening. We arrived and I quickly introduced Tom to my partner and his wife.

We picked up our race bibs and chips and walked around. Tom is a runner and runs almost every day, but he doesn't like to race. When he does race, however, he is extremely competitive! I knew what was going to happen when the gun went off. Tom bolted - there was no way he was going to let my partner beat him. His finishing time was probably the fastest he had ever run a 5K, but his age group was very competitive and he didn't place, but he did beat my running partner. At the after party he had quite a few beers, more than normal. My partner and his wife left after the awards were given out. It was getting late so we decided to stay and eat. Tom had a few more beers.

By the time we left he had way too much to drink, in my opinion. Once in the car, he locked the doors. We lived a good distance from where we were so we had to travel the main highway. On the way home he pulled off every exit and parked the car. He yelled at me demanding that I promise I would never leave him and that I would stay in the marriage FOREVER! And, he demanded that I profess my undying love for him. I told him he was acting crazy and that I would not commit to a marriage with him especially in light of his behavior. The more I refused the more pissed he got. At one of the exits I tried to call 911 with my cell because he was scaring me. I didn't know what he was going to do. He grabbed the phone and we fought. He had the doors locked and I couldn't get out. Spotting a hotel across the way, I told him that I had to go to the bathroom. He drove over but escorted me into the bathroom. He grabbed my arm and didn't let go. He took me through the side entrance so that no one would see us. He stood outside the bathroom and waited and then escorted me back to the car. I was a wreck because all sorts of triggers were going off! When we arrived home I ran to the bedroom and tried to lock the door but he was behind me and he pushed his way in. As I prepared for bed, I didn't speak to him.

Once in bed, I was hoping that it was over. No such luck. He stood by my side of the bed glaring at me. I begged him to leave me alone but instead he ripped the cover off me, grabbed me by my ankles and pulled me off the bed. My head hit the floor and I saw stars. As I came around, he had my arms pinned behind me and was yelling, "Is this what you want from him?" He was talking about Nathan, not my running partner. He kept yelling over and over as he forced himself on me. "Is this what you want from him?" He continued to yell saying no one was ever going to have me. I was so furious, I screamed "NO, because he would never treat me this way." Well, that was the last straw for him and I didn't stand a chance.

The funny thing was it still hadn't occurred to me how I really felt about Nathan. Up to that point it was nothing more than a few flirtations and conversations. After that night, I refused to let Tom kiss me. He had crossed the line too many times and this last incident was beyond the pale.

As a result of the attack and Tom's interpretation of my relationship with Nathan, I began to analyze my feelings for Nathan. Was Tom right? That following Monday I asked Nathan if he did hugs. I needed one after what had happened; I was scared and not just because of Tom's behavior. I couldn't define my feelings for Nathan. He came down to the office right away expressing concern, but once he was there I told him that I had imposed on him enough. In reality I was afraid to hug him. I wanted him to hold me so badly but standing there looking him in the eyes, I just knew if we hugged, I probably wouldn't have let go. As I watched him walk away that day, I cried for the first time in a very long time. That's when I knew I had to find out how he felt about me. A few weeks later I sent him an email. A rather childish thing to do, but my fear of confrontation hindered my ability to address the situation like an adult. I told him I was experiencing odd feelings when I was around him, feelings I had never felt before and was wondering if he felt the same. His response was shattering on so many levels. He began by saying that he had thought about it more than I would ever know, but no, he didn't. He said I needed help and listed abuse hotline numbers noting that he was very concerned for my well-being.

Prior to sending the email to Nathan, I had told Tom what I was doing. It was his insistence that there was something between us that prompted me to reevaluate my feelings for Nathan. I told Tom that I had never experienced feelings like that and I was confused. My reason for confronting Tom was simple; I wanted everything out in the open unlike my mother, who kept her affairs secret. So when Nathan responded, I told Tom what he had to say but not about the suggested counseling. Deep down I knew Nathan was right. I had known all along; I just didn't want to admit it. Tom smirked, satisfied that I had been rejected. I was devastated, absolutely devastated! Convinced that Tom was having an affair all along, and then to have him strut around at my rejection, the obvious double standard was more than I could handle. Unfortunately, Christmas was a few weeks away and I had to keep it together for the kids.

Running into Nathan was painful. I avoided him at all costs, and if I did see him, I kept my head down. It was like old times, pretend like nothing happened, compartmentalize it and forget about it. Anyway, I told Tom I didn't love him anymore, especially after the attack and that I was confused by everything that had taken place. I didn't know what healthy love was, since I didn't grow up in a loving family. Tom didn't take it well and I paid the price for several months.

Nathan's response also had confused me. I didn't think I was imagining the feelings between us, but I didn't care anymore. I fell into a deep depression. I was working full time, taking a class, and suffering from emotional stress of my marriage to Tom who, according to him, "loved me!" He was gloating over what had happened. He was always extremely jealous and possessive. It was like, you deserved it, the guy is a pussy.

I was barely functioning through the holidays. After the New Year, I decided to take two classes at a time. If I was going to change things, I had to finish my degree, which meant staying in the marriage until I could. So I began my climb to get out of the place I was in. I had to get a grip and become self-reliant and healthy.

The first week of February, Tom had a week-long conference in Florida. I had felt for a long time that he had been having an affair. The over-the-top accusations and physical abuse had accelerated after the Nathan incident, but it had started well before the August confrontation. When he came back from the conference, my suspicions were confirmed. He went into this rapid speech when he walked through the door about how loved me and wanted no one else but me, and how he was going to change and wanted to work things out, all completely out of character. His rapid speech and nervousness gave it away. He acted completely guilty. My guess is whatever was going on ended that week and he was upset.

My self-reliant and healthy attitude gave way to a full depression as I concentrated best I could on my work. I had doubled down on classes, so by mid-March I reached my limit. I was burnt out. I had taken on too much too fast to bury my thoughts about Nathan and my marriage. I decided to take a short vacation alone. Since my marriage to Tom, I had never been on a trip all alone but there was a reason for going. I was reaching nervous breakdown stage. Depression had set in and I had to do something about it. The problem was I couldn't get past the hopelessness. And so, I had started to plan my death. I had already started the process of separation from my life during the holidays. I threw out everything I ever made, all the medals I had won, the things my mother gave me. The list goes on. You see, I had already started removing any reminder of me or my family so that my kids would be free from it all. It was nothing more than garbage, rotten garbage because that's what I came from and that's all that I was, damaged rotten goods. No one could ever love me nor could I ever love, really love. That was my frame of mind at the time.

I called Tom and told him he had to come home to take care of his kids while I was gone. I was adamant to go alone. Maybe he could detect the high level of stress in my voice but I stood my ground until he agreed. I had it all planned. I flew out of the continental US to be far away. I chose Mexico. I knew if I took my life there the chances of anyone finding me would be remote.

In my hotel, I began to plan it out. I didn't want my kids to know that their mother was a depressed loser. I had brought enough pills to kill an elephant, maybe two. I planned to buy a bottle of Jack and drink them down. The trick was to do it in the ocean where eventually the tide would drag me out and I would be lost at sea forever! It was a great plan or so I thought.

I went to the beach to lie in the sun. Eventually I started talking to a woman sitting next to me. She was there on business, but had come in a day early so she was relaxing. We decided to have dinner together. I wasn't in a hurry to do the evil deed. I figured I would wait a day or two to make it look good.

That night at dinner she told me her life story, not that I wanted to hear it, and it was horrifying. Her six-year old son recently died and she was in a terrible marriage. She told me all the details about the bastard she was married to, the whole nine yards. I was stunned. All the way back to my room, I couldn't help but think about her miserable life, but she was alive and laughing! I was like, wow, this woman has been through hell and to keep her propped up she is downing all sorts of pills. Not healthy by any stretch of the imagination. The stories she told were horrific but the things she did while she was in Mexico supposedly for work were insane and beyond anyone's wildest imagination, even mine.

I thought to myself, my kids are alive and well, in fact, real well. They are both smart as hell and I've kept them from the misery of my family. I couldn't imagine one of them dying before me. What a horrific experience for a parent. The next day I got up ultra-early and went for a run passing Johnny Depp as his limo waited outside the hotel. He was there making a movie. Shortly after, I returned to the beach and thought about the night before. I walked into town, shopped a little, ate lunch at a café and walked back. All in all, I probably clocked a total of seven miles between the run and the walk. That afternoon, the kids called; they were very upset and Kylie was crying. They told me that on their way home from school (Justin was driving); they came to an intersection where an accident had just taken place. A car ran the stop sign and hit a motorcycle, sending the driver of the cycle through the air. He landed several feet away on an embankment. He was killed instantly. The kids saw him lying on the ground. Justin knew he was dead by the way his body was crumpled. It took me a while to calm them down. As I hung up the phone, it occurred to me that someone was trying to tell me something. I had to consider what was happening around me: two stories having to do with death, one of which directly affected the kids. Perhaps, maybe, just maybe, they still needed their mom. You see, I had convinced myself that I had done my job with them, but had I? They are the only reason I am still here today.

Three days later, I was on a plane heading home. I cried ALL the way! That was the spring of 2009. Once back, I buried myself in work and classes. Deep down I knew I had to get help but I still wasn't able to admit it out loud. I thought I could handle it?! Meanwhile, Nathan and I didn't speak for a year or more. I was raising the kids, taking care of the house, working and going to school. My marriage was shattered; the distance between Tom and I and the kids created an emotional divide that was devastating. When he was at home, I didn't feel anything for him. I cared about his well-being, but I didn't feel love, at least not the love needed between a husband and wife. I was going through the motions. He wouldn't talk about anything and when he did, it was always about his work, which pretty much told me where I stood in the relationship. I didn't want to have sex with him either; I went through the motions. If I didn't, he would force himself on me anyway. There was nothing there for me. No tenderness, intimacy or connection, as he had ruined that with his attacks. But again, to listen to him, he didn't understand what MY problem was. He would tell me he was a good guy.

In the fall of 2010 I was beginning to see the end of the tunnel with graduation coming in the spring semester. I felt as though I could relax. The following January marked the first time I spoke with Nathan in almost two years. Not sure what initiated that conversation but it happened. This time, I was a bit shy. Worried that I might say or do something to cause another misunderstanding, I tried to keep my distance from him because I didn't want him to think I was a stalker or worse, so communication was at a minimum. He knew I was graduating. I told him that I was graduating summa cum laude. I made it into the top ten of my class. He high-fived me! However, our relationship had suffered a severe blow. Both sides had been hurt, so I think we were treading lightly.

I was working at my marriage at least to calm things down. It had disintegrated into heated physical arguments and I didn't want the kids to witness it anymore. I tried to keep my distance from Tom, but on a few occasions, we argued so much that I slept on the couch. Tom would come from the bedroom and angrily pick me up, carry me back to the bedroom, yelling that I was his wife and I was to sleep in our bed. He never respected my need to be away from him. He held the marriage license over my head. I had signed a contract after all. Now, I ask, who reading this would want to stay with someone who talks to you like that?! Not feeling the love there! This is typical of someone who thinks of you as a possession, not a partner!

Since I had been putting my best foot forward in trying to make the marriage work, I decided we should take a trip.

I wanted to celebrate my degree, but this wasn't going to be an easy feat. Justin was already in college and working full time. Kylie was in between her junior and senior year of high school but had a full time summer job. Once the two weeks were pinned down, it was a matter of getting everyone on board. I decided on Ireland. I knew both the kids would enjoy a trip there because of their Irish heritage. Both of them were huge history buffs; one majored in history and the other minored in history. And I have always been interested in history. Tom is a walking encyclopedia. One of his best qualities is that he can recall anything. He remembers everything he reads and can recall it at random. It's a shame that he is so damn smart, but also so damn emotionally bankrupt.

August arrived and Kylie and I were excited about our trip. We had never gone overseas with the kids before, so we made arrangements to stay in several villages to ensure we were able to tour most of the country. Anticipation was high but there were underlying problems brewing. Despite all efforts to get Tom emotionally engaged in the marriage, it wasn't working. We had reached an all-time low. Justin was truly burning both ends of the candle, and he can get very belligerent without sleep. So what happened next was inevitable.

We arrived early to the airport to check-in and get through security. As the departure time arrived, the plane we were waiting for had not arrived. After the plane landed, the ground crew shut the door and announced that our departing flight had been canceled. We had to catch a connecting flight at Kennedy to Ireland. So Tom took off to another airline to secure four seats. The kids and I had to haul the carry-on luggage through the crowds to catch up to Tom. The plane was held for us.

The kids' seats were near the middle and we had the second to last row. As I sat down, Tom asked if I had his passport. I said the passports were in my bag and I would check. Tom yelled at me to check right away. I was looking through my bag and came up with everyone's but his. However, I had not reached the bottom of the bag; you know how it is ladies. Well, he hauled off and punched me, right there on the plane. I looked at him with steam seeping from every part of my head. Two seconds later, I found his precious passport, which was at the bottom of the bag. The kids did not see what he had done because they were several rows ahead of us. I've never said a word to them about it. I didn't speak to Tom during the entire flight. I wanted to crawl through the nearest hole and just disappear.

Once we reached Dublin, the tension escalated, and it wasn't just between us. Justin was in a bad mood coming off a 24/7 schedule and zero sleep, except for what he got on the plane. We weren't able to check into our hotel until the afternoon so we walked around Dublin. No matter what Tom said, Justin attacked it. Tom was getting quite nasty as well because I still wasn't speaking to him. We were there for fourteen long days.

After returning, I decided it was time to seek counseling. I was done with the marriage. Before I was able to get in to see someone, I ran into Nathan as we were leaving our building. He seemed glad to see me. When he asked how I was, I couldn't look him in the eyes. I said okay and kept moving. A few weeks later, I told him about the trip and that I had decided to seek counseling.

When I walked into my counselor's office for the first time, she asked why I was there. I said because I think I'm going crazy. I don't know what the truth is anymore. Tom had such a way of twisting things to make me feel like I was losing my mind. I told her that he punched me on a plane full of people and that was the last straw and that I needed to get myself strong so that I could do something about my marriage. At the time, I felt helpless. Add to that, my feelings for Nathan, which I wasn't able to define.

Not long after starting counseling sessions, I decided it was time to leave my job at the public relations firm. It was an extremely difficult decision for me, but not because I loved my job. Tom used my job as the reason to keep the family separated, so I loathed my job and the position I held. I knew I was ready for management but my immediate supervisor wouldn't allow me to move upward. The reason it was so difficult to leave was because I knew I would never see Nathan again. My counselor agreed that it was the best thing at the time even though I would be unemployed and dependent on Tom. I had a lot of personal work to do. Being a survivor of early childhood sexual abuse, I had very little emotional intelligence and where-with-all to get myself out of the present mess. It was finally time to face reality!

Chapter 6

DEATH OF THE COYOTE

It was fall 2011 when I started my counseling sessions. I wasn't sure what to expect but I made a conscious decision that I had to do the work to get myself wholly well if I was going to make life-changing decisions. Tom turned things around so much that often I would ask myself, am I overreacting or making it all up? I couldn't even trust my own perceptions.

When I walked through the door of my counselor's office, I didn't know what was real anymore, not that I ever did. I did have coping skills, the ones I learned to survive during my childhood and the abuse, some of them good and necessary like resilience, perseverance and humor, but others not so much like self-medication, compartmentalizing and low self-esteem. The ones I didn't have were ones I needed to live an emotionally healthy life. The first few sessions I tried to hide behind my sunglasses, but eventually my counselor Joan told me I had to remove them. She had to see my eyes; I didn't like that—it meant that someone would be able to read me. Slowly, I began to trust her and stayed with counseling because I knew I had to.

Another reason I had to leave my job was because a new

manager was hired. On his first day, he introduced himself and shook my hand. I was immediately repulsed. I suddenly felt gross and dirty, as he reminded me of someone. I couldn't put my finger on it but he was like the stereotypical sleazy used car salesman. Yuck! I knew then and there that I couldn't work with him. I managed to stay through the holidays before I finally resigned. I held off as long as I could, as the only reason for staying was Nathan. Nathan and I stayed in touch on and off after my departure. Then no communication took place. That's not to say I didn't think about him. I did.

2012 limped along. I went to my counseling sessions twice a month, sometimes more often. Fear was keeping me in the marriage; by all accounts we should have been in divorce proceedings by then. Kylie started college that fall. Her move was seven hours away from us. I was losing my biggest support aside from Justin and that was hard, but I didn't want to interfere with her decision. I tried to give both my children the support they needed to be self-reliant and I allowed them great latitude to do what they wanted within reason. Sometimes Justin would push the envelope, like the time he decided to run across the country after his freshman year in college, but that is another story!

Much to my surprise, as a coworker kept me on a list of attendees for certain work events as a contributor, that fall I ran into Nathan. He wouldn't even talk to me. Noticing his obvious discomfort, I went to my fallback position, which was to ignore and pretend it never happened. This was very upsetting. We had not been in touch for so long, I thought he would be happy to see me, but I was wrong.

Joan and I discussed this in my next session. Nathan had played a very large part in why I was there. He was the catalyst - the reason I started questioning who I was, why I was married to someone who plainly had zero respect for me and treated me like a possession, and proved over and over he didn't want to be a part of the marriage. Nathan represented all that was missing in my life. He was respectful and spoke to me as an equal. Joan was a fan of Nathan; she would say that he was her helper by holding a mirror to me. Without knowing it, he forced me to look at myself. The little girl inside me, trying to fight her way out, wanted to be heard and he read her like a book. I knew it that night we stood in the cold after that horrible lecture.

Although Nathan played a key role in my quest, he was not the central issue in my sessions. My childhood and how my marriage was a continuation of that were the primary topics. Tom's personality and abuse constantly triggered my past. I told Joan about my attempted suicide and how often I went to that dark place. In talking to her, I realized that I went to that dark place quite a lot growing up, but I never acted on it until my trip when I flew off to Mexico. I didn't act on it but I was in the process of formulating my death, which was bad enough.

Survivors of early childhood sexual abuse have a high suicide rate. Here's the deal for those of you who may not know: in the early stages of childhood, specifically between birth and the age of five, our brains are developing our cognitive, emotional and social capacities. If we are experiencing unrelenting toxic stress during this developmental stage, it will lead to life-long problems pertaining to physical and mental health. Very early intervention is vital. In my case there was no intervention and the stress was unrelenting. My cognitive thinking development was disrupted. When I finally walked through the door to my counselor's office,

I was in my mid-forties. Because my emotional intelligence was based on reaction to abuse, I had to learn how to have a healthy emotional intelligence. In essence, I had no idea how to navigate relationships in a healthy way.

On Thursday December 13th, around 11pm, I had just returned from a fourteen hour round trip to pick Kylie up from school for the Christmas break. Justin called from school. He was still in the middle of his finals. My mother, in her typical dramatic fashion, had called his cell with the phony excuse that she didn't know the number to the house. She told him to tell me that my father had died. Justin, who had never heard from his grandmother by phone, was taken aback by the call. He immediately called me to tell me the news. My first reaction was why would she tell Justin, leaving him with responsibility of passing on the bad news? Why didn't she ask for the number, if in fact, she truly had lost it? I called her to find out what was going on. We argued over her irresponsibility in the handling of the situation, which of course went over her head.

She gave me my uncle's number because he had all the information. She said that it was all taken care of and that there wasn't anything to do. I called my uncle and the truth was much worse. Not only had it NOT been handled, but no one knew what was going on. All we knew was that Dad had passed away in November. No one ever contacted the family. My uncle suggested I call another uncle because he was the one who actually spoke with the sheriff's department, so I did. He said that he received a call from Dad's neighbor who went through his mail to find any information that would lead him to a family member. They found a Christmas card from my uncle, Googled his name and found his phone number. They called and explained that

Dad had passed away in November. The neighbors assumed that the sheriff's office was searching for family, but when they didn't see anyone come to the house, and noticed the mail falling out of the mailbox, they decided to investigate. My uncle suggested I start by calling the sheriff's office. He said I needed to get down to my father's place and take care of the situation because I was the oldest sibling. Plus I was the only one the family trusted to handle it. By the time I hung up, it was after midnight and I was exhausted and there really wasn't anything I could do so I decided to wait until morning.

After digesting what had taken place the night before, I called Tom. Tom was the last one to see Dad alive. Two years before, while Tom was in North Carolina for work, he rented a car and drove to an address that came up when I Googled Dad's name. We didn't know if Tom would find him, but he did. Dad didn't even recognize Tom and answered the door with a shotgun in his hand. Tom thought Dad was going to shoot him. Tom had to tell him that he was his son-in-law. When Dad finally realized who he was, he invited him in; Tom stayed about an hour. Dad gave him a tour of his little cottage and made him a cup of coffee. Dad didn't ask anything about me or the kids. Tom was shocked that he even found him; the drive there was impossible, and in his opinion he thought that my father definitely did not want to be found. He was out in the woods on some lake in Tennessee.

I phoned the sheriff's office. The police officer I spoke with told me they had received a 911 call. When the EMTs and police arrived at my father's house, they had to break the door in. Dad was already dead, slumped over his laptop in his office chair. The EMTs tried to revive him, but they had no idea how long he had been like that. The police officer said that Dad was taken to the local hospital and from there to a funeral home. He gave me the numbers. I phoned the hospital, but the person I spoke with denied that Dad was ever there. I repeated what the sheriff said, but they couldn't explain. Then, I called the funeral home. I was told that Dad was cremated the first week of December. I asked why he was cremated. I was informed that the state will only hold an unclaimed body for two weeks and then cremate them. I couldn't believe it! They hadn't even bothered to contact his family, so how could they have determined that he was "unclaimed?"

The gentleman was sympathetic; he suggested that I call the non-profit organization that was holding his remains. Apparently this organization does this for veterans. How did they know he was a veteran? I called the non-profit. The director was able to provide more information. I asked about Dad's personal belongings. The director said that there weren't any belongings with him. The sheriff's report said that he had his wallet on him. My father always carried a large sum of money. By this time it was late afternoon and I still didn't know what had happened to Dad. I called my Uncle Pete who had moved back to New York from California. I was closer to him than my other uncles. He urged me to drive to Tennessee and find out what was going on. I knew he was right, but I wasn't happy about it. There was no way Jeff would go and I didn't trust Bill, not to mention that Christmas was the following week, and Kylie had just come home from school. That Sunday I left and I had no idea what I would find.

As I settled in for the ten plus hour ride, the emotional rollercoaster began. First off, I was dumbfounded that the hospital was denying that he was there. Why? I was mentally setting my plan of action. Uncle Pete gave me the number of Dad's neighbor, the one who had contacted our family. As I drove, I gave him a call hoping for some information. He was glad to hear from me and even more glad that I was on my way. He explained what had happened. Dad had asked the person who mowed his lawn to stop by and mow it one last time before winter. This was on November 15th. The guy showed up late afternoon on November 16th and mowed the lawn. He went to the door to let my father know he was finished but Dad didn't answer. He knew my father was home because both vehicles were in the driveway. He walked around the house looking in the windows and happened upon the office window where he saw my father slouched over his laptop. He called 911. The EMTs broke the door down and found my father already dead. They tried to resuscitate him anyway. He was then transported to the nearest hospital DOA.

Dad's neighbor, Don, waited for a few weeks for family to arrive but when it became obvious that the police had not contacted anyone, he took it upon himself to start going through my father's mail, which was falling out of the mailbox onto the ground. Don found a Christmas card from my uncle, Googled his name and found a number to call. He told my uncle that Dad had died several weeks earlier and that the house and property were sitting there with no activity. Interestingly, Don said that my father never mentioned he had children or grandchildren. In fact, Don was shocked to hear from me. He was looking forward to meeting me and would be more than happy to help, if I needed it.

It was a long drive. The scenery was beautiful even in mid-December. I arrived in Knoxville around 6 pm. The next morning I started making phone calls to get a handle on who I needed to see. The hospital was sticking to their story that Dad was never admitted there. I then contacted the sheriff's office and asked for a copy of the police report so I could track down what had happened. Next, I called the coroner's office only to be given the same runaround. I also contacted the non-profit where my father's remains were. The gentleman that I previously spoke to give me the address so I could pick up Dad's remains.

After my calls, the first thing I did was drive to Dad's house, which was an adventure of its own. The roads twisted and turned so many times, I couldn't keep track of where I was going. When I came to a dead end sign, I knew I was close. The road continued to the lake. As I drove up a steep incline and came to the cusp, what I saw didn't look like a road at all. It was more like a bike path. I was nervous as the embankment to the right went straight down to the lake. I followed the path and eventually found the house. I got out and walked around the property, but couldn't get into the house. I decided to wait for Don to come home from work. I figured he would help me break-in, which he did.

Everything was as Dad left it with the exception of what the EMTs and police moved to get him out. I walked over to his kitchen table, looked down at his paperwork; he had left his pencil and paper by the phone. In the corner near the door was a rifle. Don directed me towards the back of the house where the office was located. As I walked through his living room, I noticed how well kept it was with a large woodstove and hearth and a cedar rocker beside the fire. His antique gun hung above the mantel. As I walked through, I was flooded with emotions. I could smell him, and even the air he breathed. We stopped at the doorway leading into his office. Don pointed to his chair and said that is where they found him. The computer was sitting on his desk. I moved towards it and as I shifted his chair, I noticed the disposable adhesive electrodes left by the EMTs, one in his chair and a few on the carpet. There was paperwork on a smaller table next to the desk. There were a few rifles behind the door and boxes of bullets sat on a shelf.

    I thanked Don for helping me gain access. He was still surprised by the fact that I was Joe's daughter. He shook his head. He said he couldn't understand why my father didn't talk about me because I was such a lovely person. I said that Dad had a very bad temper, and that he was difficult to get along with and it was complicated. Don believed that because of some things that happened, which he said he would tell me later. Left all alone in my father's house, I started to weep. I felt so overwhelmed. I was flooded by so many emotions - - there are no words to describe them.

    Oddly, the first thing I did was wash the dishes left in the sink. Once I had the kitchen tidy, I walked back towards the bedrooms. The main bathroom was to the right. I found his cleaning supplies and cleaned out the sink and toilet. I continued down the hall and entered his room. What struck me most was the cross above his bed. I did a double take, why the cross? Did he suddenly find religion after all these years? I walked through the bedroom into his master bath. There on the floor was a bucket full of soapy water - - he was soaking his underwear. I dumped the water and washed his underwear, hanging it across the tub to dry. I went back to his office, looked around quickly but nothing else caught my attention.

    Uncle Pete was emailing me by the hour with a laundry list of what to do and look for while I was there. My job was to gather as much information as possible, and any paperwork from the house so that once I was home, I could go through it to determine the state of his affairs. With all that running through my head, in addition to the apparent runaround I was getting from almost every agency involved, I was in overdrive. I didn't have much time because Christmas was the following week. Kylie in particular was getting concerned because Christmas was coming and I wasn't home.

Very early the following morning, I returned to the house. I found Dad's checkbook and various other statements. Then I went to his computer to see if I could find anything. It was password protected. I tried several passwords, but no luck. I then turned my attention to the paperwork on the table next to his desk. I discovered that he was supposed to have had cataract surgery the week he died. He had lined up a friend from North Carolina to stay with him, but she canceled at the last minute so the surgery was never done. My eyes welled with tears as I thought about how lonely he must have been. I was trying to understand the solitude and the loneliness.

I then headed to the sheriff's office to pick up the police report, and then I drove to the hospital. I was trying to follow what happened and why no one contacted us. When I arrived at the sheriff's office, a clerk went over the report with me. I asked why we weren't contacted; as a result, my father was cremated before we could even have a say. I left and drove to the hospital; the reason I was hell bent on going to the hospital was because the person I spoke with at the funeral home said that there wasn't any identification on him when they received his body. I knew something was wrong because he always carried a wallet. Also the funeral director knew he was a veteran, which was the reason he was sent to the non-profit after cremation. He also mentioned his death certificate. I asked how that was possible if they didn't have his social security card or any type of identification. How could the paperwork have been initiated? None of this made sense. There were more questions than answers.

Once I found the hospital, in the next town, I went to the front desk and explained why I was there. I showed the sheriff's report that said specifically that he was indeed transported there. The head of security asked me to accompany him to his office. I didn't have a good feeling it at all. He explained that my father was in fact there, but that someone had broken into the safe and stolen all his belongings. He had the admission report with him, which by law, the EMTs signed. It listed his property that was put in the safe. When I called inquiring about my father, the department panicked. I said, "So you chose to lie and say he wasn't there?" The man was very apologetic and said that they would reimburse me for what was stolen. When I finally left the hospital, I was furious about what had transpired. In fact, I asked the guy if this was how the state of Tennessee treated all its dead. Sarcastically I said, "Remind me never to die here!"

My next stop was the non-profit organization where my father's remains were being held. This was the most surreal moment I have ever had the displeasure of experiencing. It was located in a questionable section of the city. I was all alone in a run-down neighborhood. My heart was pounding. I could feel the blood rushing through me. I entered the building and a receptionist greeted me; I told her who I was and she called the director who had been extremely helpful. He came out with a box in his hand. The box wasn't any more than 12 x 12, just a regular brown UPS box. I was shocked! It even had a shipping label on it! I just couldn't believe what I was looking at. I asked if the remains were shipped to them and they said that is how the state does it. The funeral home shipped him in this box via UPS to this organization, which in turn held the remains in storage until someone claimed them. I signed a claim form to say that I received the remains and the director put his hand on my back to give his condolences while pushing me out the door. I stood on the sidewalk outside the building; my head felt fuzzy and light, like it was tunnel vision. I vaguely remember seeing my surroundings; my eyes tried to focus on finding my car. My first thought was, here I am standing all alone in the street with my father all neatly packed in a box. A man so destructive, who caused so much pain, in this tiny box! Sad and slightly repulsed, my second thought as I walked towards the car was should I put him in the back seat or the trunk? I remember thinking, what kind of daughter am I? Back seat or trunk? Back seat or trunk? I hit the trunk button. With my father closed in the trunk, I headed back to the house to finish the task at hand. As I drove, I felt the urge to vomit; the urge didn't go away.

At the house I started to go through his mail and discovered that the bills had to be paid. Obviously the power had to stay on, but the cable and phone needed to be canceled. It was too late in the day to take care of it. I had to close down the house. I had no idea when I would be back and needed to ensure that all was secured. Uncle Pete was pretty sure Dad had money hiding somewhere because that's what he did. I thought the same, but was coming up empty.

My next phone call was to vital records to get a death certificate. One had not been issued because there wasn't enough information about my father. I provided them with the necessary information to help expedite the certificate but it wouldn't be available for a few weeks. They confirmed that the actual date of death was November 16th. He died five days before his 75th birthday.

The next morning I drove to the house and went back to work. In his office I went through his file cabinet to find anything that would help in determining the status of his estate. I found a locked safety deposit box, which I couldn't open. I searched his closet in the office. There I found his cleaning supplies and a briefcase which was empty. The closet was full of extra supplies, a jar full of silver change with Jeff's name on it and boxes on the upper shelf. Above was the access to the attic, which I climbed into to see what was up there, still looking for hidden money. I took the boxes down from the shelf to go through them. One box in particular drew my attention. It was a fairly large box wrapped in duct tape. It was apparent that Dad didn't want anyone to open it. He used to do something similar with Christmas gifts to Tom. One Christmas he hot glued the wrapping paper to a gift box, making it impossible to unwrap it.

I cut through the tape and box to open it. Inside were all the cards I had ever sent him: Christmas, birthdays, various holidays and the kids' pictures. Inside the box was another box completely wrapped in duct tape. Why would he have a box completely covered in duct tape inside another box also wrapped in duct tape? Obviously he also didn't want this to be opened. So I took the scissors and started cutting away. Inside was a large ivory Bible with gold trim like the ones used during Mass, but this was the Family Life Edition.

I wondered why he would wrap a Bible in a box and completely cover it over. On the first page was our family tree. The next page read, "This Holy Bible Presented to with my name, By Dad, January 20, 2001." It was to be my birthday present that year. I've since placed it in a cabinet in my living room with photos of him, his first bike, the navy ship he was on, and his dog tags. I sat on the floor of his office for what seemed like hours trying to decipher the message. I even phoned Joan. But true to form, I compartmentalized it. I was there on a mission and couldn't let raw emotions get the better of me.

Over the next few days, I did what I could to secure his home. I emptied the fridge and freezer of all perishable items; repaired the broken door and made sure any dishes I used were washed. I paid the bills that were overdue and paid ahead on the electric, canceling the rest. His washing machine and dryer were located in a separate building on the property, which is why he was soaking his underwear in the bathroom. The property was a bit odd in that it had three buildings on it in addition to the house.

My last night there, Don stopped by to see if I needed help. I was concerned about leaving all the guns in the house. Don offered to store them, so we took a blanket from the closet and wrapped all the guns in it. Don loaded them into his truck. I also gave him all the meat I found in the freezer that I didn't want to throw out. He took that and some other items. He had been so much help that I offered him money as well, but he refused.

The drive home was horrible. Everything was running through my head. I kept asking myself, why? Why was he so angry? What made him want to leave the only family he had to live alone? Why did he hate us so much? Why? Why? Why? It should not have ended this way but deep down I knew that this was exactly how it would end. I thought about my own family. I was glad that I had kept my distance from my father and mother to protect my kids from the craziness. But I was also sad that my kids didn't have a "normal" family unit with a grandfather who loved them. Instead, they knew very little about my family and what they did know wasn't good. I felt guilty too. I kept thinking, if only I had done something differently. If only I hadn't disagreed with him. What if I did it differently? My therapist set me straight. All victims always wonder what they could have done differently to make things better or to stop the abuse.

I got home just in time for Christmas. I was looking forward to spending it with Justin and Kylie, but there was so much going on in my head. Kylie was not happy that I had Dad in a box in the house. We had to hide it so she wouldn't see it. I had all his paperwork, laptop and the Bible. As usual we traveled to Albany. Tom's father had already passed away in 2009, so we went to visit his mother, brother, sister and nephews.

The day after Christmas, Tom and I started to go through Dad's personal belongings. Not long into the process we discovered a notarized will. He had left everything to my brother, Jeff, with my younger brother Bill and I completely left out. I was stunned. He had meant it when he said he was going to disown me. I was the only one in the family who paid him any attention. I invited him into my home when the kids were younger for holidays. I tried my hardest to get along with him. My brothers didn't have anything to do with him. In fact, with the exception of my wedding, neither one of them had seen him since high school. Not once! Yet I was disowned.

I packed up everything I took from his house, including the laptop and put it all in boxes and bags. I called Jeff and told him the news. Tom packed the items into his trunk and met Jeff at a park-n-ride off the Thruway in Albany. He handed him the stuff and walked away. A few days later I received a call from Jeff accusing me of hacking into my father's laptop. I told him I couldn't figure out the password. Jeff refused to listen to me. He called me every name in the book. He admittedly said that he had to pay someone to do exactly what he was accusing me of. He was giving me too much credit. Kylie and Justin were listening to everything he said. I was angered by the accusations and embarrassed that my kids had to hear the insanity. Shaking, I told Tom that I didn't want anything to do with Jeff anymore.

My mother, as it turns out was instigating the situation, working against me. She suggested he keep everything for himself. Up to that point, I told the family that we should split my father's estate evenly. After the call from Jeff, I lay on the floor of my living room mourning not only the loss of my father, but my whole family. I knew I had to cut them out of my life. They were toxic. It was them or me, and for once I chose ME! I had made my decision. It was a New Year and for the first time, I could breathe—really breathe. Not only did I cut them out of my life, but I gathered everything Dad had ever bought me and put everything in boxes to donate. This included the little Eskimo doll and Eskimo seal knockers that he had bought me when he was in Alaska in 1970. I had them in a shadow box. They stilled smelled like piss as that was how they would preserve the seal fur then. Also, every year for my birthday, Dad would buy me a music box. I had every kind of music box you could imagine. It was a large collection. I donated it all. The only thing I kept was a dresser he had bought Kylie when she was a baby.

I walked away from it all and never looked back. Joan agreed that it had to be done. I met with her a lot during that time, but it was all good. The family was an albatross and I finally rid myself of them.

With that resolved, I started to look for a new job. I found a project administrator position with a local company and went to work. I settled in and was managing a large project and all was well until the owner of the company lost the contract. I coasted through most of the spring and early summer with them.

On The Fourth of July I received an email from Uncle Pete. Jeff couldn't get out of his own way. His paranoia was hindering his attempts to take possession of the property. I didn't understand his problem. He had the keys to the house and Dad's car and jeep. What was the big deal? Just drive down there and live. But Jeff wasn't able to leave the house; he was a prisoner of his own demons. Uncle Pete said Jeff suggested I do what was necessary to take control of the property before the state came in and took it. We both knew what the estate was worth. Jeff could have had it all!

Tom and I contacted attorneys in Knoxville. I phoned Don and told him I would be down again. After hiring an attorney, the first step was to make me the administrator of the estate. Tom and I had to front $3,500.00 of our own money for the retainer and another $3,500.00 after I became the administrator. We also had to pay the homeowners insurance. It took over a month to get all of that set so that I could legally step onto the property.

It was mid-September. I attended a presentation that my former employer was sponsoring. I knew there was a very good chance that I would run into Nathan, but we had not spoken in over a year. I was nervous while getting ready for the evening. I was running late because my attorney for Dad's estate called at the last minute.

Nathan arrived about 15 minutes after me. As usual he kept his distance. I caught up with old colleagues and mingled. As soon as the presentation was over, I turned to pick up my coat off the back of the chair and as I looked up, there he was with a big smile. I smiled and mouthed "Happy Birthday." As I walked toward the doors, I felt a tap on my shoulder, I turned and there he was. He said he didn't read lips. I laughed and said that I was wishing him a happy birthday, and he thanked me for remembering. He asked how I was. I said I was well, but I'm not sure he believed me. Then I told him how great he looked. He was wearing a dress shirt that happened to match the eggplant colored dress I was wearing. We looked like the perfect couple standing there.

Nathan apologized for what had happened between us. He explained that he got too close too fast and had a hard time dealing with certain issues. He realized all too late, that we were friends, real friends. All that time I thought I had pushed him away. He shook his head no; that it wasn't me. At that moment, I had all I could do to hold back the tears. His apology was more than I could bear. By admitting what he had done, he was demonstrating the type of companion that I had long yearned for, someone who takes responsibility for their actions and isn't afraid or unwilling to acknowledge the hurt they caused. That had never happened in my life. No one has ever apologized for their actions towards me, ever! Nathan represented something that had eluded me all of my life. I'm not sure he recognized that.

We talked for a while about a lot of things. It had been far too long since the last time we met. He encouraged me to finish the book I was writing and recommended an editor. He knew what the book was about and the fact that I would be mentioning him (not by real name), but that didn't seem to faze him. I said no one will read it and he replied "misery loves company." He suggested I take advantage of the break I was getting while handling the estate, and finish it.

That Sunday morning, I drove to Tennessee. I phoned Nathan and left him a message thanking him for apologizing. I told him that he was the only man in my life to ever take responsibility like that and that I was truly grateful to him for being a good friend. It was a solemn drive after that.

Before I could enter Dad's house, I had to call a locksmith because Jeff had all the keys. Upon entering I discovered the flat screen TV was up against the door, and the window near the kitchen table was broken. The house smelled terrible. Jeff was supposed to take over the bills, but as it turns out, he only paid through April and stopped the electric so the house was full of mold. After discovering the TV on the floor and the broken window, I checked out the rest of his house. The liquor in the cabinet was gone as well as the dozens of boxes of bullets in his office and a briefcase. Obviously someone had broken in. I immediately called the police. I was furious! How could Jeff be so irresponsible? If I were still speaking to him, I would have killed Jeff.

I met with the attorney the next day. She handed me a box Jeff mailed to her with the keys and other papers we requested. Notably he kept Dad's ashes and the jar of silver dollars. My trip there was a bust because I couldn't prepare the house to put it on the market. I had to schedule the mold remediation for another week. Since I was already there, I made it a point to catch up with Don. It was a good thing Don still had the guns or someone would have had those too. We figured it was kids. All said and done, I was only there a few days and drove back home. The one thing I did take with me was the cross above his bed. I hung it in my bedroom between a double set of windows.

Once home, I got a new job as a contract administrator. I would start at the end of October. I wanted to give myself enough time to go back to Tennessee, take care of the mold and get the house listed. I also needed to look for an auction house to take a look at what was left to be sold.

Tom decided to go with me for the remediation and help me out because so much had to be done. He took the week off, rented a large SUV and we drove down. We spent the first day going through a lot of his papers, clothes and kitchen items. The second day Tom drove Dad's car to the Toyota dealer in Knoxville to sell it. While Tom did that, I contacted the real estate office that sold Dad the house and made an appointment for an agent to come out and get the house listed. Next, I reached out to a couple of auction houses and made appointments with them to come and take a look at what needed to be sold.

The days were long and filled with hard work. By the time we returned to our hotel room at night, I was so tired, I passed out before my head hit the pillow. We took a break when Don asked if we would like to take a boat ride around the lake. It was such a lovely fall afternoon, slightly cool, but nice and sunny. To reciprocate, we invited Don to go out for dinner. It's too bad Dad didn't realize he had such good neighbors. He alienated everyone in his life.

All in all, we stayed for a week to get the house ready for market and boxed what we could for the auction. My biggest debate was what to do about the U.S.S. Constitution model he built. It took him three years. It was proudly displayed in his living room. He loved his wooden boats. He even owned a few house boats until he couldn't take care of them anymore and then moved on to building models. This one in particular was large. I knew how much it meant to him and I couldn't decide whether to save it from being auctioned off.

As I stood in the house taking one last look before leaving, I was reminded of an incident that happened after returning from there the first time I drove down. After all the vacillating over cutting the ties with my family and making that decision, I remember waking up on a bright sunny winter morning. I lay in bed looking out at the sunrise but something was wrong, really wrong. As I looked out the bedroom window, I felt someone pushing my head into the pillow. I couldn't move. I also felt someone breathing down on my neck. I broke out in a panic. I couldn't move and it felt like there was someone behind me breathing. If I didn't move then, I felt I would always be stuck, so I got up the courage to get up from the bed and I ran all the way to the other side of the house. So, as I stood there in his house taking notice of how nice Tom and I made it look, I wondered if my father would be haunting the house, like he haunts me.

The house sold just before Christmas 2013. The closing was scheduled for early February so that meant Tom and I had to make one last run to the house to get the guns from Don and put them back in the house for the auction. We drove down mid- January, a quick weekend trip to prepare the contract for the auction. I stood in front of the U.S.S. Constitution one last time. The reason it was a difficult decision was that he spent more time building and caring for his models than he ever spent caring for us, his own flesh and blood. I let it go…

It was so final. All of Dad's things were being packed, not by me, and hauled off to an auction house. The closing on the house was the next day. Deep down I knew I would never be able to resolve my relationship with him. There were unanswered questions, emotions to be dealt with and no one to turn to, to ask why?

On February 7th the house closed. The night of February 14th there was a full moon. I arrived home from work with some daylight left. As usual Tom was out of town. I went to the window to catch the last rays of the sun before night fell. As I gazed out the window, I saw a coyote sitting between our garden and the shed. It was looking out over the valley. It stood calm and tall against as the sunset. My dog joined me in her usual spot, which was to hang over the arm of the chair while looking out the window. She spotted the coyote shortly after me and barked. The coyote turned around and trotted back into the woods. As I stood there in amazement, two deer ran across the yard into the woods behind the coyote. The coyote disappeared into the sunset. Was this another sign? Was the coyote a shape shifter? Was it my father? Sighting a coyote according to legend signifies a new beginning. I wondered what this new beginning would look like. I also wondered if there was an added significance because it was also a full moon. Time would tell. I hoped with all my heart that it meant something positive!

Chapter 7

THE AFTERMATH

One night, not long after accepting the offer on Dad's house, I was celebrating and relieving some major stress. I drank too much wine, but additionally, I was taking pain meds for a back injury I had suffered a few years earlier. Typically I avoid pain meds because I am a medicine weenie. I can't take anything without severe side effects. Even in my teen years when I was experimenting, I was the weenie in our group. It didn't take much to put me out, hence the reason I stick to alcohol as my self-medication. Anyway, I was stupid and mixed the two, and what ensued was a disaster and I ended up in the emergency room.

Because of my inability to maintain a coherent conversation, the doctors (the so-called emergency room doctors, and I use the term doctors lightly) decided I was being uncooperative and told Tom that they were admitting me to the high risk psych ward. This ward is in lock down with only the most severely mentally ill patients inside. By the time I was taken to lock down it was 5 a.m. the following morning and I had been up since 4:30 a.m. the previous day. No wonder I had been incoherent; I had been up for more than 24 hours but no one listened to either one of us.

Tom wasn't able to enter the ward, so he had to leave. I was led to a room with two beds and a woman patient who was to be my roommate.

I slept what little I could, considering the circumstances. In lock down, the mentally ill roam the halls all night with security personnel by their side. Some are extremely violent. I could hear screaming and banging all morning. Around 8 a.m. I got up and immediately went into damage control mode. I looked for a phone to call home. My first priority was to talk to my kids. I wanted them to know that it was strictly an accident. There were two "public" phones in the lobby. Tom and Kylie answered at the same time. Tom was still in shock, mortified that I was locked up in a psych ward. I was able to speak with them briefly. Tom didn't sleep either and was already in damage control. He had been gathering information on the hospital and coming up with a plan on how to get me out of there.

I hung up the phone and looked around in shock. I felt numb. One person walked up and down the hall staring off into space. Another sat in a chair chanting; yet another let out blood-curdling screams every couple of minutes. One woman was extremely violent and needed to be sent to a room where they gave her a shot to quiet her down. Others stood in a line in front of a nurse who handed them their pills. This occurred several times throughout the day. She told me get in line for my vitals and pills. I glared at her and said, "I don't take pills!" and walked back to my room.

As I looked around, I noticed the furniture in the ward was Little Tykes. I'm not kidding. I felt like I was in a preschool room. It was the big Little Tykes plastic furniture and that included the bed. No wonder my back was killing me. As I entered my assigned room, I noticed that a man, who I assumed was the doctor, was talking to my roommate so I stood out in the hall. Another nurse walked up to me and asked if I had any personal belongings. I didn't so she asked an attendant to get me a toothbrush, toothpaste, soap, shampoo, towel and washcloth. I collected what I could and waited for the doctor to finish with my roommate.

When they finished, the doctor waved me into the room. He began to ask questions, which I answered. It was obvious to him that I didn't belong there and he said as much. I told him that Tom and I tried to tell them the night before but his response was, and I will quote this marvelous psychiatrist, "Well, you bought yourself a stay here at least until Monday." Apparently this is how they treat humans: inhumanely. I had to come to grips with the fact that I was staying until Monday at the very least. As I slumped down into my bed, I had this strange feeling that I had to live this experience firsthand. I'm not sure why, but I just knew that I had to go through this. Of course, I had no idea what I was in store for.

I started drinking copious amounts of water to flush out my system. I also resolved myself to the fact that I wasn't going to be able to eat until I could get out of there. I couldn't bring myself to eat hospital food. I have a very strict diet. I eat organic food, not prepackaged foods and very rarely eat out because I have a fetish about what goes into my system. I don't drink juice or soda, which apparently were staples in the psych ward. So I skipped breakfast and lunch.

Tom arrived right at 1 p.m. when visiting hours started. He brought me some fruit and a coffee. Shockingly, that is something they won't serve on the ward. You can take all the meds in the world and drink tons of sugar via soda and juice, but coffee, no way. Apparently mental patients aren't allowed to have caffeine. But soda is allowed? I didn't have much of an appetite anyway. Tom stayed the whole hour and a half he was allowed. He wasn't in good shape. I could tell he wasn't handling the situation very well. The kids were already complaining that he was losing it at home. Later, my counselor said that it indicated how much he depended on me for everything, including holding it together. His fear of my leaving him was so great that he couldn't even bear me being locked up! Yet, I was the one locked up, the irony! My whole life is irony.

It was almost dinner time and I still had not met my roommate. She was on speed or something because the woman never sat down. She was in and out, non-stop. She did it all night too. I didn't partake of dinner that evening either. I used the time instead to reflect on the situation. Darkness was descending not only in my room but in my life. Once again, I would have to find the resolve to pick myself up, but how? I have always been an introvert. I get my energy from within and I knew I needed to focus, really focus to get through my present situation.

My roommate finally settled down enough to be formally introduced. I gave my first name and nothing else. She went full speed into her problems, which I sat and listened to as best I could. Where else was I going? I certainly wasn't going down the hall where all the commotion was happening. You see, the screaming and yelling and chanting and pacing continued all day and into the night. Earlier that afternoon, one of the women took off her clothes and ran back and forth down the hall while the attendants chased her. She ran to the lobby area where she proceeded to pound the safety glass out of the flat screen TV. She popped the bolts and shattered the glass. Others shuffled about mindlessly, stopping long enough to take their allotment of pills handed out by the nurse who always wanted to take your vitals before pushing the pills. Every time I walked by, one of them would try to take my vitals for pills. In spite of why I was there, I told them I didn't take medicine. One of the nurses resorted to taking my vitals in my room. She asked if I was on high blood pressure meds and I repeated that I didn't take meds. She gave a sigh of relief because my blood pressure was low. She thought they were giving me meds, which was why she was chasing me down for my vitals.

If you want to experience slow torture, this is it. I could see where one would slowly begin to lose their mind. I was praying for the evening to end as I sat and half listened to what my roommate was saying. As she spoke, I looked at her, really looked at her and she was a mess. My initial thought was that she was a nuisance. Eventually, that first impression began to shift as I grew concerned; I could see she was really struggling. From what I could gather, her husband was the reason she was there. She confided that when released, she would go to a home and then to her parents who lived out of state. I went to bed early knowing the night would be long and interrupted (and it was). I awoke in the middle of the night to a man standing over me, who was one of the patients they allowed to wander the halls. I panicked as he stood there staring at me. I thought, I damn well better not get sexually assaulted while here, or the hospital would rue the day they admitted me. I couldn't sleep after that. The next day I was forced to participate in a group session. Another patient didn't like the questioning by the attendant, so she jumped on her and wrestled her to the ground. As others jumped up, my chair became wedged and I was caught between the chair and wall. Doesn't this sound familiar? Does it remind you of a certain bar scene? The meeting ended with incident, where the attendant suffered a bite wound on her hand.

Monday came and true to form, Tom arrived prepared for a fight. And that he did. He pounded on the glass of the admittance office until they listened to him. By late afternoon I was released. Due to his paranoia, Tom planned the escape by telling me to wait in the lobby while he got the car. He really thought that they would change their minds as I was leaving. His plan was to drive by and I was supposed to run and jump in. So as he drove by the entrance, I jumped in the car (our Bonnie and Clyde moment) and we never looked back. Funny thing was I had to run and jump with bare feet because in his rush, Tom forgot to bring me my shoes and it was freezing out that day!

The experience was an eye opener. All those years I thought I was crazy, but after having spent three days with what I would classify as mentally ill patients, I was as far from crazy as you could get. I wasn't imagining anything at all. My experience taught me to pay attention to my head and heart. I knew then that I was right about Tom. He was having affairs and trying to make me think I was imagining them. I knew that I would have to have that conversation with him. Additionally, I felt that God had a purpose for me that I somehow had not fulfilled. I'm supposed to accomplish something, but I'm just not sure what that is. Let's face it, I used up my nine lives long ago and had just used one more, so there had to be a reason for living! So I waited to confront Tom. The trauma from my little vacation was too much for the family to handle. Everyone needed time to digest what had just taken place. I decided it was best to leave it alone for a while.

By spring of 2014, I was ready to confront Tom. I discussed my marriage options with Joan, my counselor. She referred me to a mediator who I contacted. Tom was not happy that I went to great lengths to betray him, in his words. But, I needed the support so that he couldn't twist things. We went to the initial meeting and the mediator first spoke with both of us, and then separately. I went last. When I was in her office, she asked why I was still with him. In her opinion, he was going to do whatever I said. Whether we were to stay together or divorce. He was emotionally detached. She didn't think it would matter one way or the other to him.

When we were both in the office, Tom told her that he didn't want a divorce and that he wanted to work on the marriage. He held that position over the next several months. The truth of the matter was Tom didn't want a divorce because he didn't want to pay me spousal support. He said that I was ruining his life and that if I followed through, he would have to work until he was 80. The mediator told him if he didn't want a divorce he would have to start being active in working on the marriage.

Tom had no idea what being active meant. When he left for work on Monday mornings, he would forget everything discussed over the weekend. Friday nights when he returned, it was like starting from scratch. He is the type of person who ignores uncomfortable situations hoping they take care of themselves. The truth of the matter was, while he was telling the mediator and me that he didn't want a divorce and wanted to work on the marriage, he was actually seeing another woman. In fact, the mediator had suggested he seek counseling on his own to work on his issues. He went to one she recommended but he didn't like her. After two visits, he smugly said that he didn't need counseling, and that it was my opinion he needed it. That's when I knew, one hundred percent, he was with another woman. She was boosting his self-esteem. He was cocky and invalidating our marriage.

This went on all summer. He would tell the mediator that he didn't want a divorce but he wasn't working at the marriage either. He resorted to accusing me of things, too. One time while we were out jogging, he accused me of treating him like a sugar daddy. I damn near killed him on the spot. I couldn't believe what I was hearing. Then he would ask me if I had guys over to the house when he was gone, namely Nathan. I asked if he was crazy. Why would I do that? How? I worked, took care of the house, and the kids were around. And, we were married. Yes, I will not lie, I thought about it—a lot! But I would never do that especially with someone like Nathan. In my opinion, if you like someone and respect them, the last thing you would do is compromise them. But Tom was all about compromise. He always compromised us, which was a sure sign of disrespect.

In the meantime, Kylie was still in school and Justin had moved back home. They knew how miserable I was and wanted me to end the marriage. Now, Tom always left his cell phone on the bedroom dresser on the weekends. He didn't want anyone from work to contact him. One Saturday morning, I remember looking at his phone as I left the bedroom. Later I was stripping the bed to wash the sheets and I noticed his cell phone wasn't on his dresser, which was odd because he never took it anywhere with him. Back in the kitchen, I asked him where his phone was. He looked me in the eyes and said that it was on the dresser. I shook my head. I asked again where it was and he swore that it was on the dresser. I then asked why he was intentionally lying to me. He walked away towards the bedroom. Because I had a straight shot from the kitchen, I shifted slightly to watch what he was doing. He paced the bedroom floor, then walked up to his dresser and pulled the phone from his pocket and put it there.

When he came back out to the kitchen, I asked why he was intentionally lying. He said he wasn't. So at this point in time, my coyote was a trickster, thinking he could outsmart me. We argued about it until early afternoon when he came up to me and said, "If you must know, I was looking at ESPN." I wanted to pummel him right on the spot! How dare you insult my intelligence like that.

That Monday he was headed to New York City. He was leaving as I was pulling in from work. His flight was a later one but he was all dressed up. Immediately, I knew something wasn't right. He said he was dressed in case he ran into some of the guys from work. But he was also renting a car, which wasn't typical. I felt sick inside. I knew that he was with someone and the cell phone incident confirmed it. He was probably texting her all weekend. But because he was so far away, I knew I was going to have a hard time proving it.

When he came home that Friday night, I asked him why he was hiding his cell phone from me and why he had me locked out of it. It was just the two of us in the house since the kids were gone. Saturday morning, we argued some more. About mid-morning he brought me his cell phone and said here, if you must look at it. I took the phone and went right to his trash file and there were emails from his lover. Obviously he forgot to empty his trash. As I started to read, he jumped over the back of the chair hitting me from behind. We flew forward onto the floor and he landed on top of me. We both fought for the phone. Once he had it, he ran into the other room. I was still on the floor. I knew I hurt something but I wasn't sure what. I was so upset that when I did get up, I walked to the bedroom and started to pack some clothes. I was leaving. Tom followed me into the bedroom, shut the door, and then locked it. He told me I wasn't leaving the house. That was ridiculous. "You attack me and then tell me I can't leave?" He held me in the bedroom for an hour before letting me out. He then followed me everywhere I went. He took the car keys to both cars and hid them so I couldn't leave.

We argued the rest of that day. I demanded that he tell me who his lover was and he insisted nothing was going on. Then as I was printing something from my computer, I happened to notice the email on the back of the paper. Tom always put used paper in the printer. I read that he was asking someone if it was her Harley sweater. She responded yes, that she ought to know. I went ballistic. He said he didn't know what that was about. I was like, yeah right! If he didn't tell me what was going on, I was going to call his boss and let him know that Tom was using his work phone and email to carry on an affair with someone in the industry, which would have gotten him fired. I did that on purpose because to Tom, his job is his life. Any threat to his livelihood was the end of the world for him. He begged me, "Why would you do this to me?" I was like, really? YOU did this to yourself, you asshole!

The next morning, Sunday, I found an opening where I could sneak out the door and go get help. I made a run for it, but Tom caught me and dragged me back to the house. The irony was he had to rely on me to give him a ride to the airport to pick up a car that night, so he was going to have to let me out sooner or later. We argued the rest of that day. I did drive him to the airport, but when I got home, I parked the car and locked the doors just so he would stay away from me. I put my head down on the steering wheel and cried. When he pulled in behind me, he saw me sitting there with my head down and thought I did something to myself. He ran over to the car and started shaking it and yelling at me. I looked up, like what the hell is your problem? I opened the door and he yelled at me thinking I did something to myself. I said I needed time to think, that's all. I was going to call his boss in the morning. He begged me not to ruin his life. I said I didn't care about his life anymore and went to bed.

The next morning I contacted the mediator and told her to initiate the paperwork for the divorce. To date, we were only counseling with her and discussing the ways in which we would separate our estate. Tom called me from his car while he was in a TV station parking lot. He was there to record something for work. He told me who the woman was and again begged me not to call his boss. I agreed for the moment. Naturally, I immediately looked her up. She worked for one of the firms in their industry. Tom travels a lot to New York City. In fact, probably forty percent of his work involves her group. And to top it off, she was eight years my senior. When Tom came back that Friday, he said that he broke it off and wanted to work on fixing the marriage. I didn't believe him, but the holidays were coming and I didn't want to disrupt that with the kids. I tried to make nice for the holidays but I tortured myself for staying, knowing there was no good reason to do so. I beat myself up constantly.

During the holidays, Tom seemed to be more focused on us, but then the travel picked up again in January. One of my biggest gripes was that he was never home and that he was stealing my life from me by expecting me to just wait around for him to "visit" as the kids called it. He told me I was exaggerating so I decided to keep a calendar of all the days he wasn't home. I put a big red X on the days he was gone. We limped through winter but I wasn't noticing any "work" on Tom's part to stabilize an all too deteriorated relationship. To make matters worse, he didn't even contact his own kids! Not even to say hello, touch base with them or let them know he loved them. I scheduled another meeting with the mediator the first of March. Before the appointment, I sat Tom down and showed him the calendar. From January to that day almost every day was marked with a red X, very few were open. He did a double take and couldn't believe it. I looked at him and said it was NOT my imagination that he was gone all the time.

We went to our appointment, which was the first step in detailing how the separation agreement would read. There was a breakdown of our accounts, possessions and the percentage of his income I would receive. At the end of the meeting, the mediator asked for $1000. Up to that point, I had been paying for our visits, which typically were $150 or $250. Now we were actually writing our settlement and heading towards a divorce. When we left, I thought he was going to yell and scream, but he didn't. Our conversation instead consisted of whether or not this was something we wanted. Other than that, it was a quiet ride home.

A week or so after our meeting, Tom was back in New York City. He left at night again and was dressed in a suit. I thought it was strange and asked why he was dressed up. Again, he said he wanted to be dressed in case he ran into some of the guys. He was also renting a car, something he didn't typically do because he usually took the subway to the hotel. He said he had an offsite meeting. The next night he called as he was driving to have dinner with the "guys." He said one of them lived on Long Island, and so they were going there for dinner. I didn't believe the story. I waited a few hours and sent him a text, which he didn't respond to. I tried to call him, no response. I waited until 10:30 and called him again, no response, so I phoned the hotel where he was staying and asked for his room, no answer. I went to bed, but woke up at midnight. I called his phone again, but no answer. I called the hotel, but no answer. I left a message on both phones asking where he was. I went back to bed, got up at 1:30 and tried both phones again, no answer! I left a message on both. Went to bed again, woke at 2:30 and tried again. No answer. I tried again at 3:30, no answer. The house phone rang at 4:15 with a very wide awake Tom yelling at me saying he didn't hear the phone ringing and that he just happened to roll over and notice the message light on the room phone. I said do you really think I'm supposed to believe that? You didn't hear either phone? Fuck you!

Kylie was coming home the following week for her birthday. I tried to hold it together for that, but the tension between Tom and me was obvious. I had all I could do to not show my total contempt for him. Not only that but I had purchased tickets months prior for a concert in April that I wanted to go to, which meant we had to keep it together as the concert was out of town. In May, Kylie was graduating from college, which was another trip out of town for several days, and Justin would be riding with Tom and me. Kylie's graduation was the turning point not just for me, but the kids too. The drive there wasn't too bad. Justin slept most of the way because he is always burning both ends of the candlestick.

But what happened when we were there was the last straw. It started out fine, but then as we drove to our hotel in Montreal, Kylie and her boyfriend were following us. Tom took the wrong exit off the highway and we immediately got lost in the city. Tom went into panic mode. When he does that, he can't hear what you say to him at all. Kylie was trying to keep up behind us but it was rush hour and she quickly lost sight of our car. I asked Tom to give me his phone so I could GPS the hotel and get a new set of directions, but he wouldn't let me take it. In fact, he was fighting me for it. Then, Justin yelled, "You are going to get us killed." Justin asked for the phone so he could get the directions. Tom refused to give it to him. We finally made him stop so that Kylie could catch up to us. By the time we finally found the hotel, everyone was so pissed at Tom, they wanted to punch him. Kylie's boyfriend was so upset he parked her car in the middle of the road and immediately walked off so that he wouldn't punch Tom. In the lobby while Tom was checking us in, Justin said that Tom was definitely hiding something on his phone. Justin and Kylie knew about the other woman because I told them what happened that previous October. Justin said it was definitely the other woman and that I should just finish the divorce papers and get it over with. No one would talk to Tom after that and Kylie's graduation was the next morning. What a disaster. She was so upset that her father ruined her graduation. She was crying, but Tom who is self-centered didn't see what the big deal was.

When we got home, I phoned the mediator, and told her I wanted to proceed with the divorce. We scheduled an appointment for the following week. When we entered her office, a man pulled Tom off to the side presenting him with the divorce papers to sign. The mediator took me into her office while the guy was going over the paperwork with Tom. Tom eventually walked in with a red face. We discussed how the accounts were to be broken down and how much my spousal support would be. Then she asked for another $1000.00. If looks could kill, I would be dead. When we left, Tom immediately accused me of setting him up. I didn't know she was going to do that, but he didn't believe me.

After that we went back and forth. One minute he was trying to work at the marriage and then other times he seemed like he was somewhere else. He made several trips to New York City and rented cars with the excuse that he had offsite meetings, but I knew better. We did have several intense conversations on the weekends, but when he walked out on Monday mornings it seemed like everything we talked about went out the window. July 4th was around the corner and he was leaving for France. His company was based there and always had this meeting over our 4th of July break. I went a couple of times and we took the kids once and spent time with our friends in Normandy, but all things considered I was not going this time. Tom had arranged to take off the Friday before leaving because he was going to be gone for a week. That morning as we were talking he said for the first time ever that he wanted a divorce. My heart sank because it was then I knew she was the force behind his decision. We were both driving to work at the time and I couldn't believe he waited to say that as he was preparing to leave. I asked if she was going with him, he said no. We agreed this was pretty bad and that we should be taking the time to discuss it.

Not much was resolved, but while he was in France I hired a private investigator. Initially, the P.I. did surveillance when Tom was in the Rochester office, but I insisted he was having an affair in New York City. Then came all the proof I needed. It was in August and our 29th wedding anniversary was the following month. Unbeknownst to me, Tom was making plans for us to go to the coast of Maine. I presented him with some of the evidence I had. I held back information because I knew I would need it down the road. The look on his face was priceless! There was no way he could turn it around and claim I was imagining this. He asked what I wanted to do. The answer was simply to finish the divorce process and get it to the judge. We were in the middle of several revisions that needed to be addressed. I asked him if he was in love with the woman and if so, did he have plans to move in with her or marry her. The evidence I found was that he had asked her to commit. Then he told me about the weekend he had planned to spend with me. I guess I just didn't get it. Your spouse has an affair and supposedly has feelings for this other person, yet he makes arrangements for an intimate weekend? Does this make sense to anyone? Anyone?

I told him I wasn't going to celebrate another anniversary with him. He had already put a deposit down and purchased the plane tickets for the trip as a surprise. He only did it because the woman turned him down. In the correspondence between him and his lover, he had asked her to commit to him and she responded that that was ridiculous.

That week I scheduled another appointment with our mediator. In talking with my counselor, Joan, I made the decision to go to Maine, but not to celebrate. I specifically told Tom that I was going only because it was a trip I wanted to take. We had been together long enough that we could certainly go as two people who in spite of all that was happening shared many interests and the coast of Maine was one of them. We cared about each other because we had been together for so long, but love was a different story. Joan was a little critical of my decision but she also knew how much I loved the coast. As long as I set boundaries for the trip it would be okay.

While there, Tom came down with a stomach virus, but in my opinion he was sick about what he had done. We were in a beautiful inn on one of the most beautiful bays on the coast of Maine. On Saturday morning Tom turned to me and said he wanted to go to counseling to work on being a better person and husband. I was shocked. It was the first time he would willingly do anything to help himself and the marriage. WOW! I couldn't believe what I was hearing. I asked if he was kidding. He said he had been thinking about it since I confronted him with the proof of his affair. I didn't believe him. Tom would tell me what he thought I wanted to hear and then would forget about it. The difference this time was his tone. He sounded like he was giving up the control of his emotions, which he worked tirelessly to keep inside. The weekend was good. He was on his best behavior. The fact that he was sick probably had something to do with it.

After our trip, I continued to work with our mediator on the revisions so we could get it to the judge. Meanwhile, I found a male counselor for Tom. Joan (my counselor) felt that I didn't have anything to lose by waiting to see what he did. It was our joint opinion that Tom wouldn't follow through. So despite the fact that we had the paperwork near ready for the divorce to proceed, I agreed to hold off and see how Tom did with counseling. My curiosity was piqued. His first appointment was in October. We went over key issues that I felt needed to be addressed plus any he could think of. He was reluctant because he doesn't like to talk about his feelings, and he already had two bad experiences with the previous female counselors.

After his appointment, he wanted to share what they covered and that it wasn't as bad as he thought it would be. I had my doubts that he was being honest with the counselor, but I was glad that he scheduled another appointment for November. For someone as emotionally shut down as Tom, it was impressive that he chose to go back. So I told myself to be a little patient with him. I contacted our mediator and told her that he was in counseling and I was waiting to see what would come from of it. After his sessions, I would ask "What have you learned, Dorothy?" (As in Dorothy from the Wizard of Oz)

The holidays came quickly and it seemed Tom was genuinely trying to work on some things, but I was cautious for obvious reasons. I knew he wasn't telling his counselor the truth about his relationship with the other woman and I knew he wasn't telling me the truth either. I was sure because I had the report from the private investigator and I was holding out on information to see if he would really come clean. He said he didn't want to get kicked out of the family and that he wanted the marriage to work, but that only happens when there is mutual respect and trust—neither of which existed. So my gauge to see if I would stay and work it out was to see if he would come clean. I needed it to come from him.

In the spring we traveled to Switzerland for Tom's work. Justin came with us. We had a good time, as even Justin was on his best behavior. We went to Mont Blanc and did a day trip to Milan, on Holy Thursday. I insisted on going to Santa Maria delle Grazie. There was no way we would see the Last Supper but we did see the church.

It was mid-summer when I returned to see Joan; we discussed how Tom was still going to counseling. I told her I didn't know how to proceed. I knew he wasn't telling the truth about his relationship with the other woman but he was making progress in other areas. Joan suggested I make an appointment with a marriage counselor. If we went, we would know if it was going to work out or not. She gave me the name of a male counselor. I contacted him and scheduled an appointment. We went and I jumped right into explaining everything. He usually likes to start out slowly, but I laid everything on the table.

Right after our first visit with the marriage counselor, Tom received word that he had won the highest award his industry offers and that the award would be presented at the company's annual meeting in November. I told him I would like to go and he wanted me to be there. There was only one major problem. It was the organization he worked with in New York City, and the other woman would be there. I wasn't sure how I would handle the situation. As November drew near, I felt my body and mind kick into high gear. We had only been to one marriage counseling session, and I was still of the opinion that the divorce should go through. Tom was too quick to work on finding my replacement instead of repairing our relationship. He intentionally deceived me and made me think I was losing my mind. How do you forgive that?

The week of the award ceremony, Tom went ahead of me as he had meetings leading up to the event. I worked the first half of the week and took the rest off. I flew in the night before. Tom had to attend meetings the day of the event, so I went for a four-mile run and had an appointment for a manicure and pedicure. After my spa visit, I went out to the pool and soaked up a little sun before getting ready for the evening. Tom's meetings ran late and when he arrived back at the room, he was in a rush to get ready. As a result, we were among the last to arrive at the cocktail party. I wore a black skirt coupled with a white silk sleeveless blouse with black satin trim, and a pair of low black suede pumps with one front cross strap embellished with large rhinestones. Basically it was a very dressy tux. As we walked into the cocktail party, I took a deep breath. We turned the corner and all eyes were on us. Tom quickly led me to a group of people to introduce me. Because we were late, we didn't get much time to mingle and I'm sure that was by design.

Because Tom was the recipient of the award, we were seated at the front table with the CEO, vice president and general manager of his company, all there to see him get the award. At the table were other top CEOs with their spouses. The conversation was good, but because we were at round tables, I felt very uncomfortable because I knew Tom's lover was in the room and she could see me, but I didn't know where she was. We sat through several speakers pontificating about their achievements and the industry, and the usual pat on the back crap. Then Tom and the other recipient were presented their awards. After the ceremony, the vice president of Tom's company came over to me and thanked me. He said that if I didn't do what I did, Tom wouldn't be able to do his job. Tom had one of the worst travel schedules in the company. I agreed and thanked him for recognizing my sacrifices as well.

As we stood there, people were coming up and shaking our hands to congratulate Tom. I turned to shake hands with a woman who introduced herself. It was her. Now I could have had many reactions, but in a split second, I composed myself, smiled and thanked her. She turned to Tom and congratulated him with a smile. Tom looked shell-shocked but shook her hand. We quickly moved away as the rest of the table decided to have a nightcap at the bar.

While we were seated in the bar talking with various people, the woman walked in and sauntered over with a drink in her hand. She hung off of every guy she touched. She was wearing a gaudy patterned blouse that hung below her cleavage for all to see, with an equally loud skirt and big gaudy jewelry all over. Actually, she was the complete opposite of me. I'm petite, I don't wear make-up and I don't wear big gaudy jewelry. She made her way around the table until she got to me. She butted in on the conversation we were having with another couple and started telling some story about how her prior supervisor wrote her up for drinking at ten o'clock at night at one of these events. She was looking for sympathy. She insisted upon involving me in the conversation all the while looking me up and down. Eventually she walked away and made her way around the rest of the tables. I was insulted that Tom would even have anything to do with someone so fake and even more insulted that he thought she was my replacement! When we finished our nightcap, we went to our room. I was in no mood to deal with him after meeting her.

The next morning Tom had to attend meetings until noon, so I went for another run and started to pack. Before making arrangements for the award ceremony, we had decided to take some time to drive up the coast and stay in a hotel we like. I like it because I can sit on the balcony and watch the dolphins play in the water. The drive was quiet as I sorted the thoughts in my head about what I learned the night before. And, yes, for someone who was basically done with the man, I was hurt or I should say my ego was hurt. The drive was longer than we anticipated so we didn't arrive until dinner time, but that was okay because we were able to get into a restaurant that we really enjoy. The next day was a beautiful, hot day, not what we expected at all. I found myself in my favorite shop not too far from the hotel to buy some swimsuits. We spent the whole day at the pool. It was very relaxing and we enjoyed ourselves. We went back to the same restaurant that night because it's our favorite and we can't get good Cuban food at home.

When we returned, I had several talking points for our marriage counselor who we were going to see after the long break. He was very sympathetic to the situation and gave us a few things to work on before our next appointment. However, during that appointment and all subsequent appointments with him, Tom swore up and down that he didn't have anything to do with the woman sexually. Once again we were nearing the holidays and I hate to bring up conflicts during that time, so I held my concerns until after the New Year. Tom was still making additional appointments with his counselor, which was totally unexpected.

I started to push Tom for the truth. Since Tom had started his counseling, his statement to me and our marriage counselor was that he just wanted to move forward. Well, I couldn't do that! You can't move forward if you don't understand what happened or confront the truth; you just can't. There is no basis to continue the marriage if there is no truth, something we never had. So I was grasping at straws. I had nothing other than the few times that he really came forward and supported me through family crises. Joan asked me if the few times were worth a lifetime. It was the end of March, when Tom finally came out and admitted that he had been to the woman's house. We discussed this during our counseling session. I had dug my feet in about this trust issue and I had stated all along that I knew Tom was lying and now it was coming out. The counselor said Tom hurt me in my most vulnerable spot, trust! Given my past, I didn't trust anyone. They have to earn it from me. The counselor looked right at Tom and asked if there was anything else, and if there was, he should spill it now because if he didn't the marriage would be over. Tom was adamant that he had only been to her house once for a couple of glasses of wine, no sex. I didn't believe that for a moment because you see, I knew there was more.

This brings us to the summer of 2018. How should I describe the summer of 2018? I can't say that it was the worst summer of my life because having read this so far you can see that I've had so many bad experiences that it would be difficult to classify it as the worst. On an emotional level, it was very stressful. The first and second week of June, I had had enough with Tom and his "let's just move forward" crap. I knew there was more to the story and it just so happened that he was in New York City that week. It was his second home. Tom was at dinner with the president of another industry association. He sent me a text early in the evening and I responded. Then he sent me a text a little later around 8:30. His text indicated he probably had too much to drink. I waited a bit to give him time to get back to the hotel because that was his intention. When I sent him a text, he didn't respond. So I waited a little longer and called his phone, no answer. I waited a little longer and tried again, still no answer. Finally I called the hotel and asked for his room. We made a deal in marriage counseling that he had to let me know his room number so that I could track him down if necessary. There was no answer in his room. Has anyone heard this story before? Naturally, I felt I was being played again. You know the old saying, fool me once shame on you, fool me twice shame on me. But, in our relationship it was more than twice already. My anger was justifiable. I beat myself up for allowing myself to get conned, again!

When he arrived home the next night we argued loudly. The neighbors across the ravine heard us. I finally pulled out all the stops and told him I had proof that he was there more than once and that they were having a sexual affair. The argument went on for several hours. Then, Tom finally admitted to being there several times. I flipped, I absolutely flipped. So much so that Tom called our counselor the next morning and asked for an emergency session. I was walking out, I was done. The counselor agreed to get us in the next day, which was a Saturday. When I told the counselor what happened, I thought he was going to get up out of his chair and smack Tom. You could tell he was restraining himself. Tom had lied to the counselor and me, but I doubt Tom understood the severity of that. Our counselor finally understood why I kept saying I didn't trust Tom. It was because I knew. The conversation was directed at Tom the whole time. In fact, every time I tried to talk, the counselor put his hand up to shush me. Then the counselor asked him if there was anything else, anything to add to what happened. Tom answered that he had also taken her out to dinner. The counselor asked if that was all. Then he asked Tom why he was admitting that he had taken her to dinner and Tom said that it was the right thing to do. I was livid.

Little did I know other equally serious issues were brewing; I received a phone call from my cousin the following week. My brother, Bill and his partner had moved back in with my mother. Between them, they stole all her savings. They took her checkbook and forged her signature. They stole over $30,000 and cut her off from the family by taking her phone away. They pawned her diamond ring, good sterling silver and my grandmother's china, and crashed two vehicles. My mother had to borrow money from Jeff to buy another car. Bill and his partner lost custody of their kids, and had been arrested. So it was clear that they were back at their old habits, only worse now. They were on heroin. Bill took everything in the house and sold it. What he didn't steal and sell, he broke.

I couldn't feel sorry for my mother. It wasn't the first time Bill had done this. If she had pressed charges the first time, maybe Bill would have recovered, but she always coddled him because he was illegitimate. My cousin also suspected that Bill was abusing my mother too. To prove to my mother that she had to press charges against Bill, my cousin had a friend of hers run a check on him and found out he and his partner were wanted on several charges in different states. Knowing that I had walked away several years ago, my cousin tried to make me feel guilty by saying it was my responsibility to take care of my mother and begged for me to step in.

Reluctantly, I called my mother at her job, but when she picked up the phone, I couldn't control my anger and I issued an ultimatum. I told her she could either accept my help and it would be done my way or reject my help and I would walk away, period. She chose not to accept. I told my cousin there was nothing I could do because she didn't want my help and I didn't want to get involved. My cousin would not let up on me. Additionally, I learned that my brother Jeff was still living in the old farm house with the foundation collapsing around him (a metaphor of his life), a prisoner of his delusions and paranoia.

The trifecta that same week was an email I received from Nathan. He and his longtime partner had eloped and were moving out of state. With all that had taken place up until that very moment, when I got the news, I broke down and cried. In fact, I cried uncontrollably for three days. No matter which way I turned, it was bad. Nathan had raised the bar for me. While Tom and I sit in our marriage counseling sessions, I think about that. Would Tom ever get close to that bar? Would he learn to be respectful? I want my partner to be genuine, not someone who tells lies and invalidates my feelings. Through years of counseling and my relationship with Nathan, I had come to understand what I was looking for in a relationship. Missing in my life were truth and respect! Tom is showing signs that he in fact wants to work towards those elements. He just doesn't know how to do it, according to our marriage counselor. Our counselor is of the opinion that Tom has opened up considerably in acknowledging his bad actions. Tom has been willing to listen to alternative ways to function within our marriage.

As for Nathan, our relationship has endured despite the limitations. I had asked him long ago to take the lead because I grew up without the basic knowledge of relationship boundaries and there were no boundaries in my marriage. He had to be the grownup in the room. Admittedly it was difficult at times, kind of like the child who has been told to keep her hands out of the cookie jar. It was tempting. The packaging was appealing and the stuff inside was genuine and I could only dream about it. He stood his ground for me. At a time when I was fighting to keep my head above water, Nathan was my float - a buoy, but it was up to me to land safely. I thank him daily for being so strong and standing by me when I needed a man to do so. I am forever grateful to him. We keep in touch to this day.

Through all of my counseling I've discovered that family is the most important thing to me. Tom and I built something together that neither of us had growing up, and if we can resolve the issues that keep us from experiencing a healthy relationship, then I am all for it. But time will tell. I hang in there because I know that there is a better person inside him. He has demonstrated this periodically throughout our marriage. How many people would sit there and hand write out old family recipes for their spouse? He stood by me when my father passed and again when I landed in the psych ward. However, I fear there is more that has not come out yet. My fear has kept me in the marriage. My fear keeps me from trusting that this time he will change. However, I am open to accepting that he can change. Coyotes are highly adaptable and who's to say that the trickster isn't changing for the good?!

Author's Note

This book is not about outing anyone; therefore, names, cities and states have been changed to protect those involved. This book is about navigating our way through the path of victimhood with all its pitfalls. This is about survivors who have to endure a great deal of pain throughout our lives. We were changed forever by abuse. But there is hope. There are many options today, such as counselors and help lines. You have to be willing to seek that help. You have to be willing to stop the cycle of violence. Life is about choices and just because we were dealt a shitty hand doesn't give us the right to deal someone else one too. The purpose of this book was to say, yes, my life sucked, in my opinion, but I made a conscious decision to change course. It takes a lot of hard work, I will not lie, but it has been worth it. Additionally, I tried to stay as close to timelines and sequences as possible. I did write about many of the powerful events that occurred as an adult, but I didn't keep a daily journal.

 The body never forgets trauma. For most of my life, I have suffered from back pain. Most recently, I developed a cyst on my spine, in the place where I had been shoved into the steel bar under the cot where I was sexually abused as a young child. After surgery, I should fully recover from this latest setback. How ironic that my spine will be held together with steel pins. It is a stark reminder that our bodies never forget.

It has been three years since Tom and I began marriage counseling. He continues to see his personal counselor as well. There are those that would say I should have left and never looked back and in the heat of the moment, I would not disagree. However, I would like to think that in staying and working through our issues, both personal and as a couple, I will accomplish something I wasn't able to do in my past.

Marrying Tom was not an accident. Tom, much like my father, was emotionally detached, unable to talk about his love for me. Tom would buy me nice things in lieu of becoming emotionally close. Dad did the same. Dad was never able to express his love, but would instead make sure that we had a good Christmas. Maybe it was his way of expressing his remorse. I tried in vain to reconcile my relationship with Dad throughout the years. I longed for the father I never had and with his death, it is now an impossibility.

In staying in our marriage and fighting for respect and a healthy relationship, I would like to think in some way, I could accomplish what I wasn't able to accomplish with my father. Instead of running, which would have been easy and typical, I stuck it out and fought for what I knew deep down Tom was able to provide. He just needed guidance in how to express his emotions in a healthy way, guidance that I begged him to get for years, but he refused. It all boils down to this: you have to want to be a better person and seek out guidance in order for it to work.

Do I trust him? I needed Tom to be genuine, to admit what he had done. Instead, it was worse than pulling teeth. He even lied to our marriage counselor. I need to decide if he is someone who is genuine and cares about my well-being or someone who invalidates me and lies, unable to face the consequences of his own actions. I do think I am capable of trusting him someday. According to our counselor, as long as I am open to the possibility of trusting Tom, then we could work towards a healthy marriage, so long as Tom continues to be honest. Trust is a very fragile thing for me. A childhood fraught with untrustworthy adults makes for not a good marriage, especially when one marries someone who runs in the opposite direction to avoid the necessary emotional conversations. But through counseling, Tom has come to realize that trust is a trigger for me and that it is something earned. He has risen to the challenge and works every day on this because he wants to be trustworthy. Our relationship has grown stronger as a result and I believe, the healthiest it has ever been.

Acknowledgements

I would like to thank my counselor, who is one of my biggest fans. She has the patience of a saint and has stood by me through some very trying times.

My Son and Daughter. They endured not only my mid-life crisis, but the emotional rollercoaster I was on as I worked through my past and a failing marriage – a double whammy for sure. I'm so proud of them.

My dear friend J. A true gift and I am forever grateful.

My editor, who despite her battle with breast cancer sifted through my thoughts and kept me on track. I wish her well.

And my husband, who upon reading the final draft of this book apologized for providing so much material. He offered to help make last minute edits and insisted that I publish my book knowing full well that he doesn't "look good." Imagine my surprise.

Reference Page

Cadieux, Charles L. 1983. *Coyotes: Predators & Survivors*, New York: Stone Wall Press.

Dobie, J. Frank. 1949. *The Voice of the Coyote*. Boston: Little, Brown and Company.

Grady, Wayne. 1994. *The World Of The Coyote*, The Sierra Club. Originally published in Canada by Greystone Books, a division of Douglas & McIntyre Ltd., 1615 Venables Street, Vancouver, British Columbia V5L 2H.

Ryden, Hope. 1975, 1979. *God's Dog: A Celebration Of The North American Coyote,* Published by Coward, McCann & Geoghegan, Inc., 1975 and by The Viking Press and Penguin Books 1979.

www.ingramcontent.com/pod-product-compliance
Lightning Source LLC
LaVergne TN
LVHW021713060526
838200LV00050B/2648